EASY GUITAR
WITH NOTES & TAB

GREAT AMERICAN GOSPEL FOR GUITAR

T0045082

ISBN 978-0-634-01589-2

HAL•LEONARD®
CORPORATION
7777 W. BLUEMOUND RD. P.O. BOX 13819 MILWAUKEE, WI 53213

Visit Hal Leonard Online at
www.halleonard.com

CONTENTS

STRUM AND PICK PATTERNS

This chart contains the suggested strum and pick patterns that are referred to by number at the beginning of each song in this book. The symbols ⊓ and ∨ in the strum patterns refer to down and up strokes, respectively. The letters in the pick patterns indicate which right-hand fingers plays which strings.

p = **thumb**
i = **index finger**
m = **middle finger**
a = **ring finger**

For example; Pick Pattern 2
is played: thumb - index - middle - ring

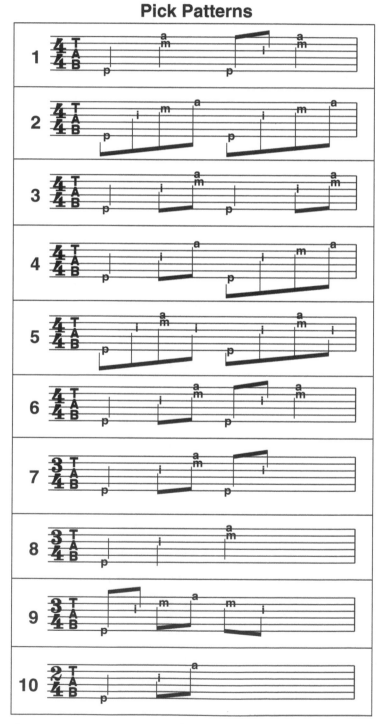

You can use the 3/4 Strum or Pick Patterns in songs written in compound meter (6/8, 9/8, 12/8, etc.).
For example, you can accompany a song in 6/8 by playing the 3/4 pattern twice in each measure.
The 4/4 Strum and Pick Patterns can be used for songs written in cut time (¢) by doubling the note time values in the patterns. Each pattern would therefore last two measures in cut time.

Amazing Grace

Words by John Newton
Traditional American Melody

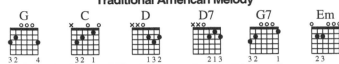

Strum Pattern: 7
Pick Pattern: 7

Additional Lyrics

2. 'Twas grace that taught my heart to fear,
   And grace my fears relieved.
   How precious did that grace appear
   The hour I first believed.

3. Through many dangers, toils and snares,
   I have already come.
   'Tis grace has brought me safe thus far,
   And grace will lead me home.

4. The Lord has promised good to me,
   His word my hope secures.
   He will my shield and portion be
   As long as life endures.

5. And when this flesh and heart shall fail,
   And mortal life shall cease.
   I shall possess within the veil
   A life of joy and peace.

6. When we've been there ten thousand years,
   Bright shining as the sun.
   We've no less days to sing God's praise
   Than when we first begun.

All the Way My Savior Leads Me

Words by Fanny J. Crosby
Music by Robert Lowry

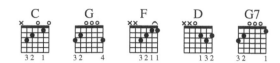

Strum Pattern: 9
Pick Pattern: 7

know what e'er be - fall me, Je - sus do - eth all things

well; for I know what - e'er be - fall me, Je - sus

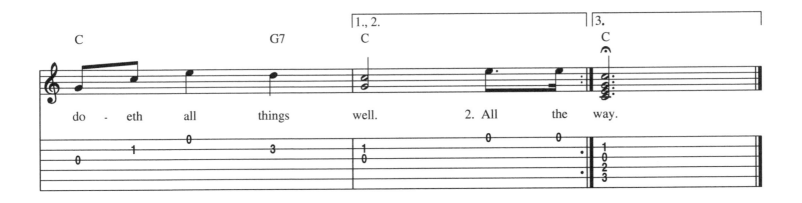

do - eth all things well. 2. All the way.

Additional Lyrics

2. All the way my Savior leads me; cheers each winding path I tread,
Gives me grace for ev'ry trial, feeds me with the living bread.
Though my weary steps may falter, and my soul athirst may be,
Gushing from the rock before me, Lo! A spring of joy I see;
Gushing from the rock before me, Lo! A spring of joy I see.

3. All the way my Savior leads me; O the fulness of His love!
Perfect rest to me is promised in my Father's house above.
When my spirit, clothed immortal, wings its flight to realms of day,
This my song through endless ages: Jesus led me all the way;
This my song through endless ages: Jesus led me all the way.

Are You Washed in the Blood

Traditional

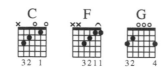

Strum Pattern: 3, 4
Pick Pattern: 1, 3

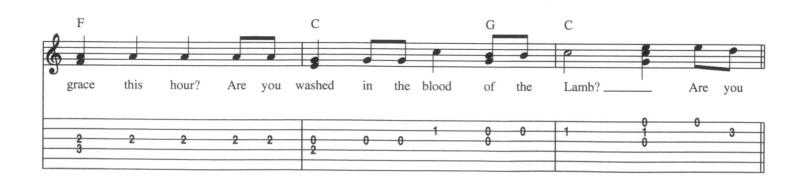

Chorus

washed (Are you washed?) in the blood, (In the blood.) in the soul cleans-ing blood of the

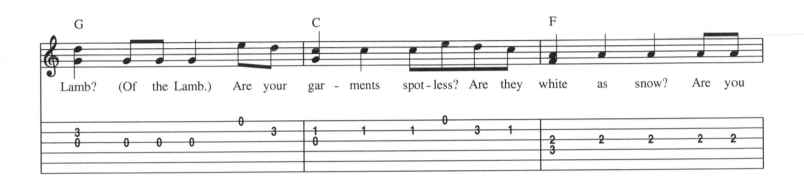

Lamb? (Of the Lamb.) Are your gar - ments spot-less? Are they white as snow? Are you

washed in the blood of the Lamb?_____ 2. Are you Lamb?_____

Additional Lyrics

2. Are you walking daily by the Savior's side?
   Are you washed in the blood of the Lamb?
   Do you rest each moment in the Crucified?
   Are you washed in the blood of the Lamb?

3. When the Bridegroom cometh will your robes be white?
   Are you washed in the blood of the Lamb?
   Will your soul be ready for the mansions bright,
   And be washed in the blood of the Lamb?

4. Lay aside the garments that are stained with sin,
   And be washed in the blood of the Lamb;
   There's a fountain flowing for the soul unclean,
   O be washed in the blood of the Lamb!

At Calvary

Words by William Newell
Music by D.B. Towner

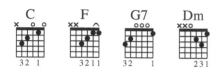

Strum Pattern: 3, 4
Pick Pattern: 1, 3

Verse
Moderately

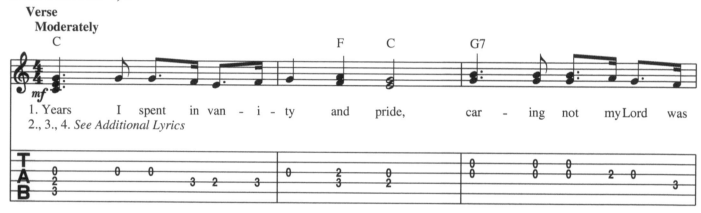

1. Years I spent in van - i - ty and pride, car - ing not my Lord was
2., 3., 4. *See Additional Lyrics*

cru - ci - fied, know - ing not it was for me He died on

Cal - va - ry. _____ Mer - cy there was great and grace was free,

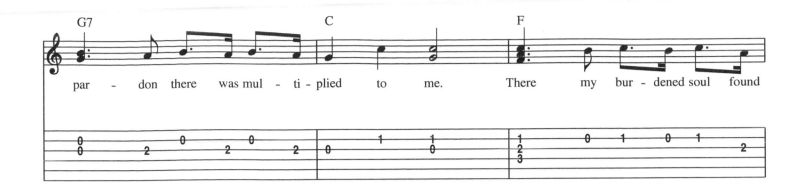

par - don there was mul - ti - plied to me. There my bur - dened soul found

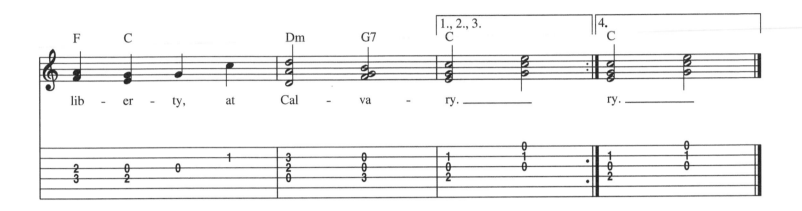

lib - er - ty, at Cal - va - ry. _____ ry. _____

Additional Lyrics

2. By God's Word at last my sin I learned;
   Then I trembled at the law I'd spurned,
   Till my guilty soul imploring turned to Calvary.

3. Now I've given to Jesus ev'rything,
   Now I gladly own Him as my King,
   Now my raptured soul can only sing of Calvary.

4. O the love that drew salvation's plan!
   O the grace that brought it down to man!
   O the mighty gulf that God did span at Calvary!

At the Cross

Text by Isaac Watts
Music by Ralph E. Hudson

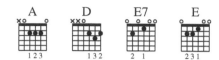

Strum Pattern: 2
Pick Pattern: 4

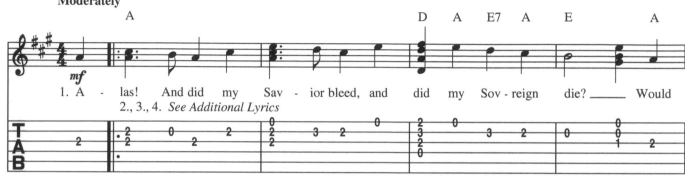

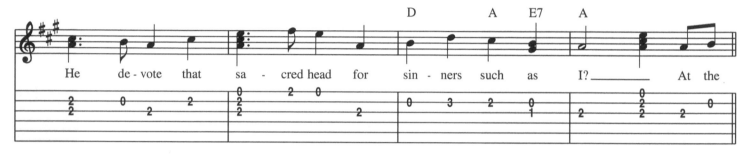

Additional Lyrics

2. Was it for crimes that I have done He groaned upon the tree?
   Amazing pity! Grace unknown! And love beyond degree!

3. Well might the sun in darkness hole and shut His glories in,
   When Christ, the mighty Maker, died for man the creature's sin.

4. But drops of grief can ne'er repay the debt of love I owe:
   Here, Lord, I give myself away; 'tis all that I can do!

Blessed Redeemer

Words by Avis B. Christiansen
Music by Harry Dixon Loes

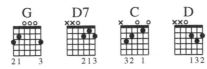

Strum Pattern: 8
Pick Pattern: 8

Verse
Moderately Slow

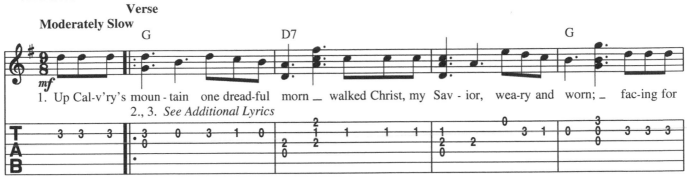

1. Up Cal-v'ry's moun-tain one dread-ful morn _ walked Christ, my Sav-ior, wea-ry and worn; _ fac-ing for
2., 3. *See Additional Lyrics*

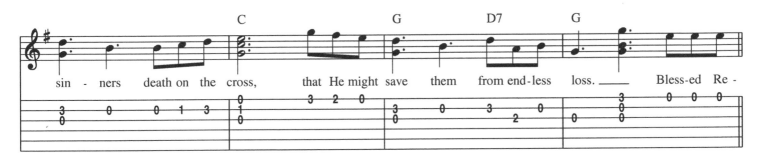

sin - ners death on the cross, that He might save them from end-less loss. ____ Bless-ed Re -

Chorus

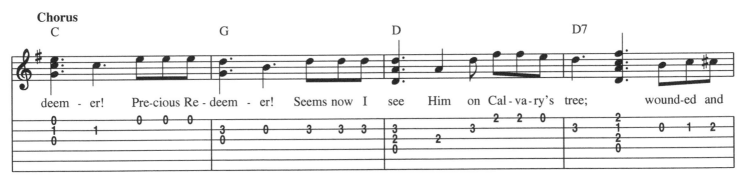

deem - er! Pre-cious Re - deem - er! Seems now I see Him on Cal-va-ry's tree; wound-ed and

bleed - ing, for sin-ners plead - ing, blind and un - heed - ing, dy-ing for me! ____ 2. "Fa-ther, for- me! ____

Additional Lyrics

2. "Father, forgive them," thus did He pray,
E'en while His life-blood flowed fast away.
Praying for sinners while in such woe,
No one but Jesus ever loved so!

3. Oh, how I love Him, Savior and Friend!
How can my praises ever find end?
Through years unnumbered on heaven's shore,
My tongue shall praise Him forevermore.

Blessed Assurance

Lyrics by Fanny Crosby and Van Alstyne
Music by Phoebe P. Knapp

Strum Pattern: 8
Pick Pattern: 8

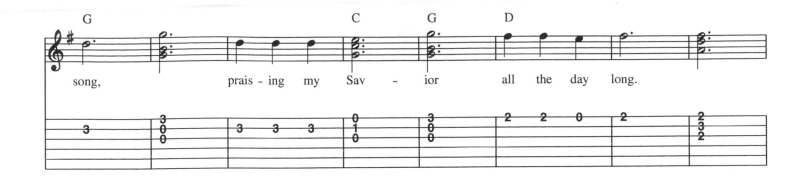

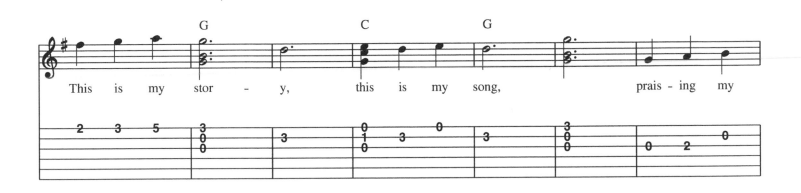

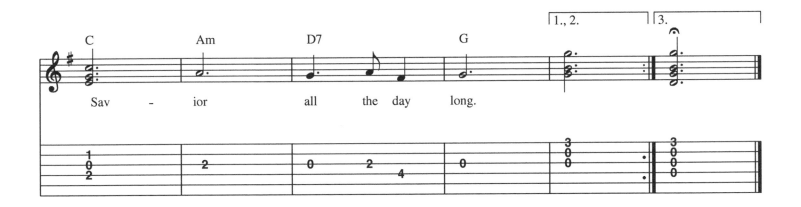

Additional Lyrics

2. Perfect submission, perfect delight,
   Visions of rapture now burst on my sight.
   Angels descending, bring from above
   Echoes of mercy, whispers of love.

3. Perfect submission, all is at rest.
   I in my Savior am happy and blest.
   Watching and waiting, looking above,
   Filled with His goodness, lost in His love.

Blessed Be the Name

Words by William H. Clark (verses) and Ralph E. Hudson (refrain)
Composer Unknown
Arranged by Ralph E. Hudson and William J. Kirkpatrick

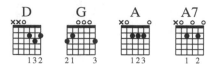

Strum Pattern: 3, 4
Pick Pattern: 1, 3

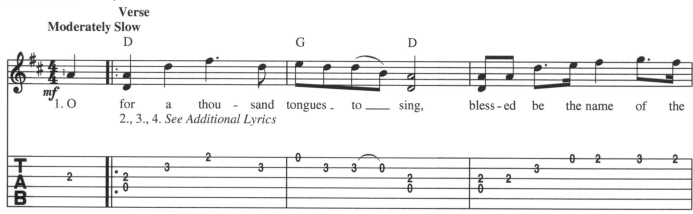

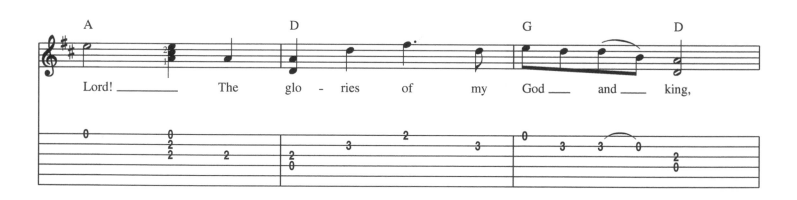

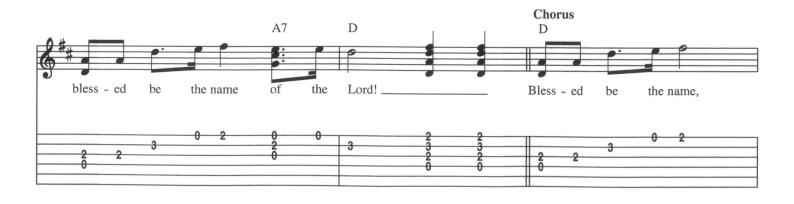

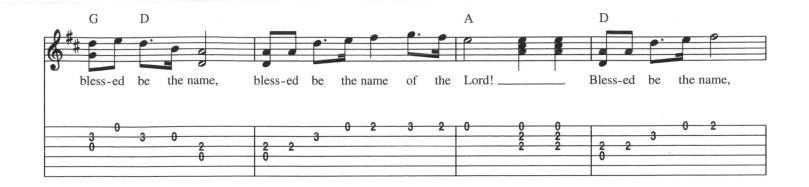

bless-ed be the name, bless-ed be the name of the Lord! _____ Bless-ed be the name,

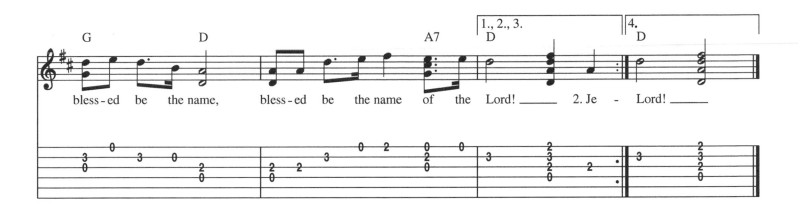

bless-ed be the name, bless-ed be the name of the Lord! _____ 2. Je - Lord! _____

Additional Lyrics

2. Jesus, the name that calms my fears,
   Blessed be the name of the Lord!
   'Tis music in the sinner's ears,
   Blessed be the name of the Lord!

3. He breaks the pow'r of cancelled sin,
   Blessed be the name of the Lord!
   His blood can make the foulest clean,
   Blessed be the name of the Lord!

4. I never shall forget that day,
   Blessed be the name of the Lord!
   When Jesus washed my sins away,
   Blessed be the name of the Lord!

Brighten the Corner Where You Are

Words by Ina Duley Ogdon
Music by Charles H. Gabriel

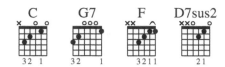

Strum Pattern: 1
Pick Pattern: 2

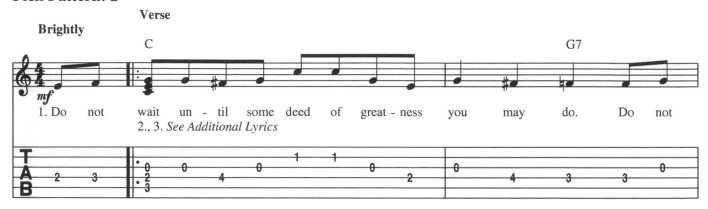

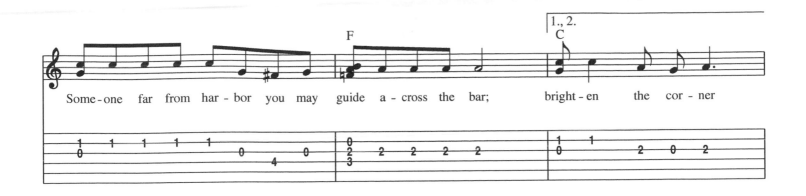

Some-one far from har-bor you may guide a-cross the bar; bright-en the cor-ner

where you are. 2. Just a - bright-en the cor-ner, bright-en the cor-ner,

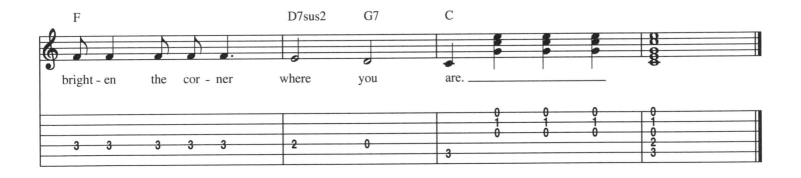

bright-en the cor-ner where you are. _____

Additional Lyrics

2. Just above are clouded skies that you may help to clear.
   Let not narrow self your way debar.
   Though into one heart alone may fall your song of cheer;
   Brighten the corner where you are.

3. Here for all your talent you may surely find a need.
   Here reflect the bright and morning star.
   Even from your humble hand the bread of life may feed;
   Brighten the corner where you are.

Church in the Wildwood

Words and Music by William S. Pitts

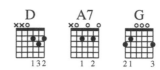

Strum Pattern: 3, 4
Pick Pattern: 1, 3

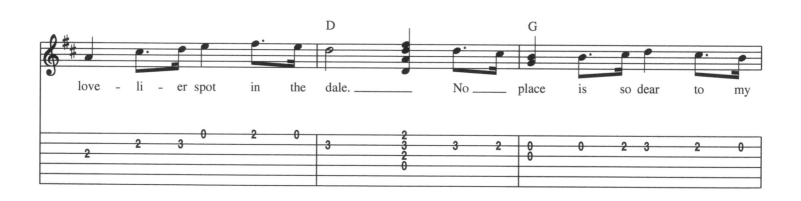

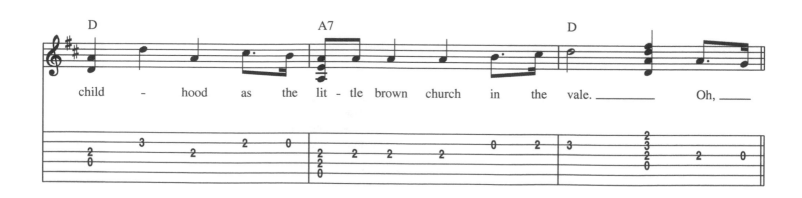

Chorus

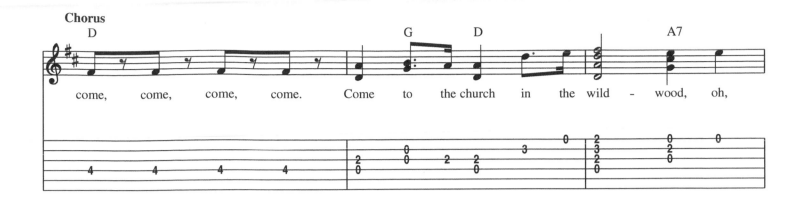

come, come, come, come. Come to the church in the wild - wood, oh,

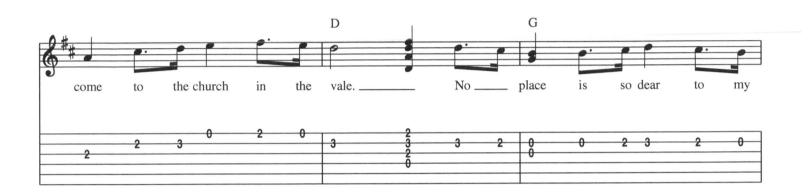

come to the church in the vale. _____ No _____ place is so dear to my

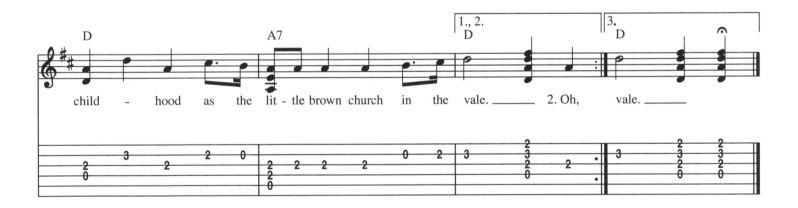

child - hood as the lit - tle brown church in the vale. _____ 2. Oh, vale. _____

Additional Lyrics

2. Oh, come to the church in the wildwood,
   To the trees where the wild flowers bloom,
   Where the parting hymn will be chanted;
   We will weep by the side of the tomb.

3. From the church in the valley by the wildwood,
   When day fades away into night,
   I would fain from this spot of my childhood;
   Winging way to the mansions of light.

Do Lord

Traditional

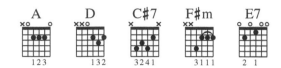

Strum Pattern: 3, 4
Pick Pattern: 1, 3

Verse
Joyfully

1. I've got a home in glo - ry land that out - shines the sun, _____
2. *See Additional Lyrics*

I've got a home in glo - ry land that out - shines the sun, _____

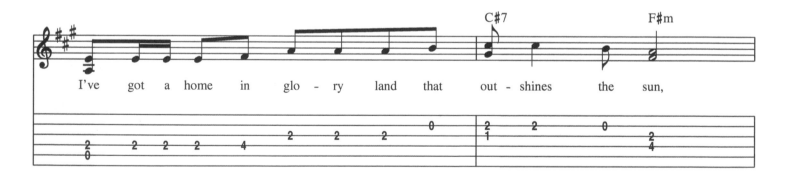

I've got a home in glo - ry land that out - shines the sun,

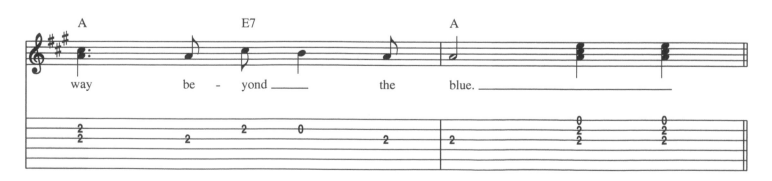

way be - yond _____ the blue. _____

Chorus

Do Lord, O do Lord, O do re-mem-ber me. Do Lord, O do Lord, O

do re-mem-ber me. Do Lord, O do Lord, O do re-mem-ber me,

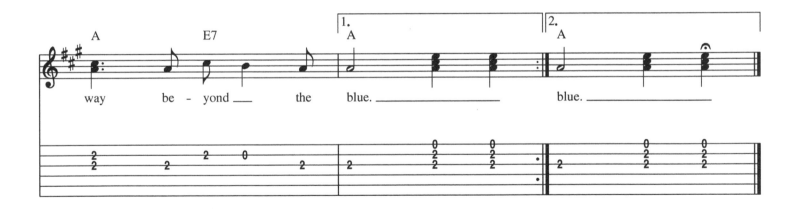

way be - yond ___ the blue. _____ blue. _____

Additional Lyrics

2. I took Jesus as my Savior; you take Him, too.
   I took Jesus as my Savior; you take Him, too.
   I took Jesus as my Savior; you take Him, too.
   While He's calling you.

Does Jesus Care?

Words by Frank E. Graeff
Music by J. Lincoln Hall

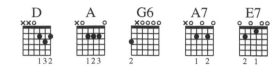

Strum Pattern: 8
Pick Pattern: 8

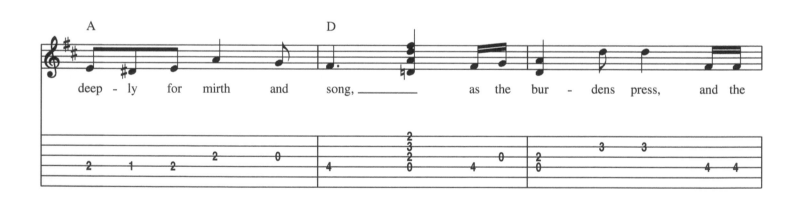

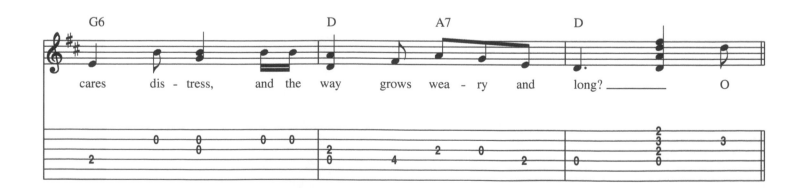

Chorus

yes, He cares, I know He cares; His heart is touched with my

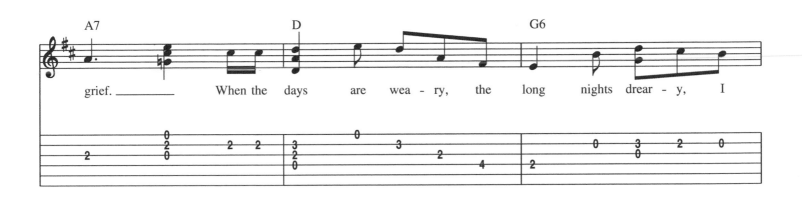

grief. _____ When the days are wea - ry, the long nights drear - y, I

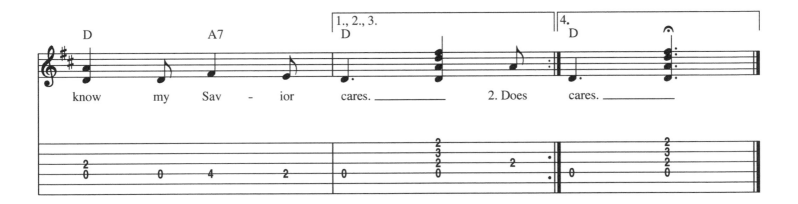

know my Sav - ior cares. _____ 2. Does cares. _____

Additional Lyrics

2. Does Jesus care when my way is dark
   With a nameless dread and fear?
   As the daylight fades into deep nightshades,
   Does He care enough to be near?

3. Does Jesus care when I've tried and failed
   To resist some temptation strong,
   When for my deep grief I find no relief,
   Though my tears flow all the night long?

4. Does Jesus care when I've said, "Goodbye."
   To the dearest on earth to me,
   And my sad heart aches till it nearly breaks,
   Is it aught to Him? Does He see?

Down at the Cross

Words by Elisha A. Hoffman
Music by John H. Stockton

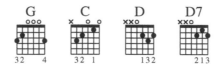

Strum Pattern: 3, 4
Pick Pattern: 1, 3

Verse
Brightly

1. Down at the cross where my Sav - ior died, _____
2., 3., 4. *See Additional Lyrics*

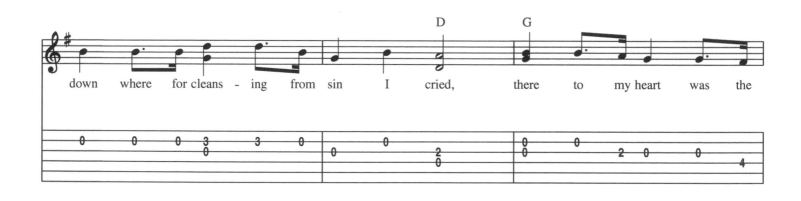

down where for cleans - ing from sin I cried, there to my heart was the

blood ap - plied. _____ Glo - ry to His name! _____

Chorus

Glo - ry to His name, _____ glo - ry to His

name! _____ There to my heart was the blood ap - plied; _____

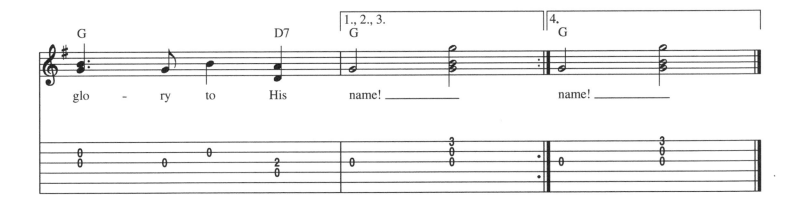

glo - ry to His name! _____ name! _____

Additional Lyrics

2. I am so wond'rously saved from sin,
   Jesus so sweetly abides within,
   There at the cross where He took me in.
   Glory to His name!

3. O precious fountain that saves from sin,
   I am so glad that I entered in,
   There Jesus saves me and keeps me clean.
   Glory to His name!

4. Come to this fountain so rich and sweet,
   Cast thy poor soul at the Savior's feet,
   Plunge in today and be made complete.
   Glory to His name!

Footsteps of Jesus

Words by Mary B.C. Slade
Music by Asa B. Everett

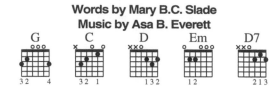

Strum Pattern: 2, 4
Pick Pattern: 1, 3

Verse
Moderately Slow

1. Sweet - ly, Lord, have we heard Thee call - ing, "Come, fol - low Me!" _____
2., 3., 4. *See Additional Lyrics*

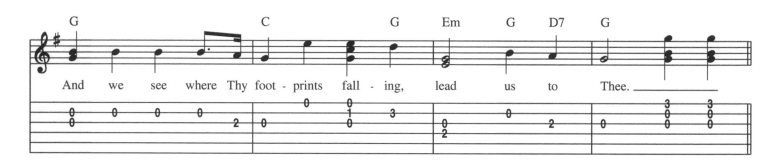

And we see where Thy foot - prints fall - ing, lead us to Thee. _____

Chorus

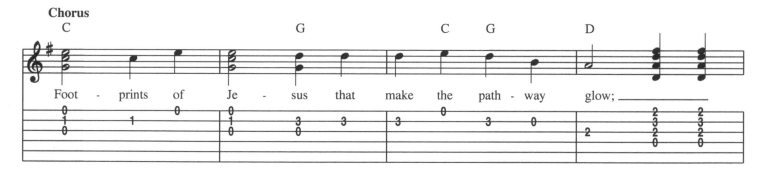

Foot - prints of Je - sus that make the path - way glow; _____

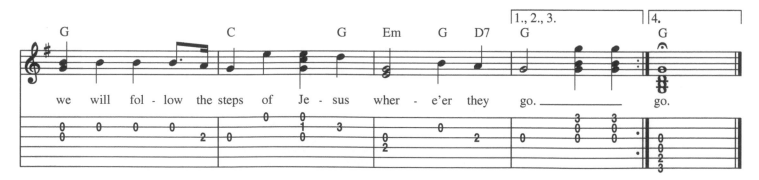

we will fol - low the steps of Je - sus wher - e'er they go. _____ go.

Additional Lyrics

2. Tho' they lead o'er the cold, dark mountains, seeking His sheep,
Or along by Siloam's fountains, helping the weak.

3. If they lead thro' the temple holy, preaching the Word,
Or in homes of the poor and lowly, serving the Lord.

4. Then at last, when on high He sees us, our journey done,
We will rest where the steps of Jesus end at His throne.

Give Me That Old Time Religion

Traditional

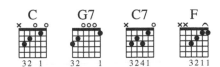

Strum Pattern: 3, 4
Pick Pattern: 1, 3

1. Give me that (4.) old time re-li-gion, give me that old time re-
2., 3. *See Additional Lyrics*

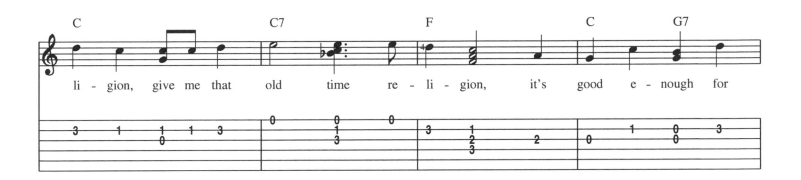

li-gion, give me that old time re-li-gion, it's good e-nough for

me!   2. It was me!   4. Give me that me!

Additional Lyrics

2. It was good for our fathers,
   It was good for our fathers,
   It was good for our fathers,
   And it's good enough for me!

3. It was good for our mothers,
   It was good for our mothers,
   It was good for our mothers,
   And it's good enough for me!

Glory to His Name

Words by Elisha A. Hoffman
Music by John H. Stockton

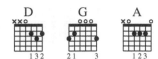

Strum Pattern: 3, 4
Pick Pattern: 1, 3

Verse
Moderately Slow

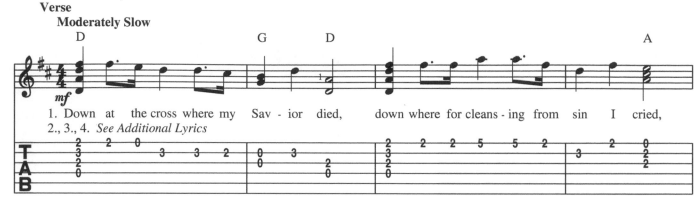

1. Down at the cross where my Sav-ior died, down where for cleans-ing from sin I cried,
2., 3., 4. *See Additional Lyrics*

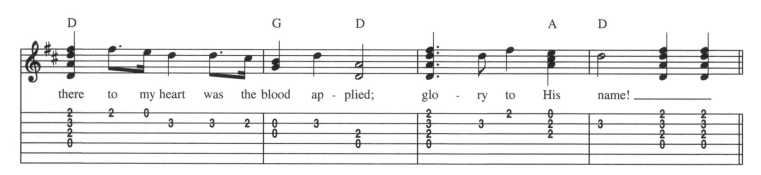

there to my heart was the blood ap-plied; glo-ry to His name! _____

Chorus

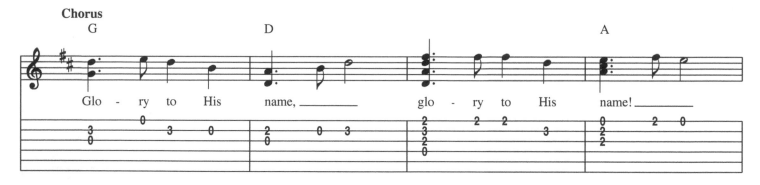

Glo-ry to His name, _____ glo-ry to His name! _____

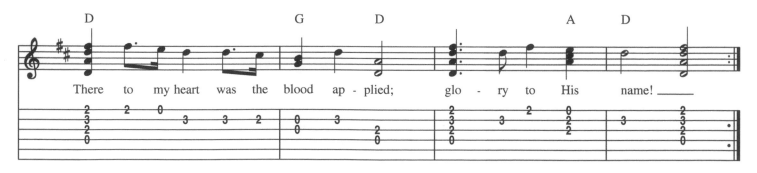

There to my heart was the blood ap-plied; glo-ry to His name! _____

Additional Lyrics

2. I am so wondrously saved from sin,
Jesus so sweetly abides within;
There at the cross where He took me in;
Glory to His name!

3. O precious fountain that saves from sin,
I am so glad that I entered in;
There Jesus saves me and keeps me clean;
Glory to His name!

4. Come to this fountain so rich and sweet;
Cast thy poor soul at the Savior's feet;
Plunge in today and be made complete;
Glory to His name!

God Will Take Care of You

Words by Civilla D. Martin
Music by W. Stillman Martin

Strum Pattern: 3, 4
Pick Pattern: 1, 3

Verse
Warmly

1. Be not dis-mayed _ what-e'er be-tide, God will take care of you; _
2., 3., 4. *See Additional Lyrics*

be-neath His wings _ of love a-bide, God will take care of you. _

Chorus

God will take care of you, through ev-'ry day, o'er all the way;

He will take care _ of you, God will take care _ of you. _ you. _

Additional Lyrics

2. Through days of toil when your heart doth fail,
God will take care of you;
When dangers fierce your path assail,
God will take care of you.

3. All you may need He will provide,
God will take care of you;
Nothing you ask will be denied,
God will take care of you.

4. No matter what may be the test,
God will take care of you;
Lean, weary one, upon His breast,
God will take care of you.

Hallelujah, We Shall Rise

By J.E. Thomas

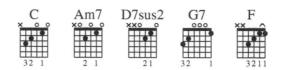

Strum Pattern: 3, 4
Pick Pattern: 1, 3

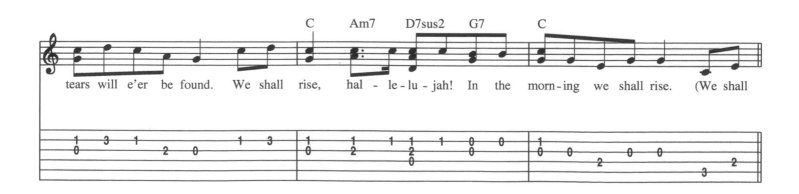

Chorus

rise.) Hal - le - lu - jah! (We shall rise.) A - men. (We shall rise.) Hal - le - lu - jah! In the

res - ur - rec - tion morn - ing when death's pris - on bars are bro - ken, we shall

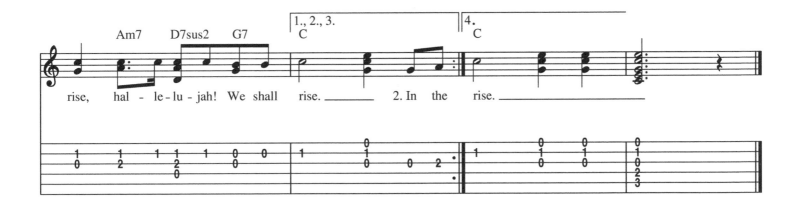

rise, hal - le - lu - jah! We shall rise. _____ 2. In the rise. _____

Additional Lyrics

2. In the resurrection morning, what a meeting it will be!
   (We shall rise.) Hallelujah! We shall rise.
   When our fathers and our mothers and our loved ones we shall see!
   We shall rise, hallelujah! In the morning we shall rise.

3. In the resurrection morning, blessed thought it is to me;
   (We shall rise.) Hallelujah! We shall rise.
   I shall see my blessed Savior who so freely died for me.
   We shall rise, hallelujah! In the morning we shall rise.

4. In the resurrection morning, we shall meet Him in the air.
   (We shall rise.) Hallelujah! We shall rise.
   And be carried up to glory to our home so bright and fair.
   We shall rise, hallelujah! In the morning we shall rise.

Have Thine Own Way Lord

Words by Adelaide Pollard
Music by George Stebbins

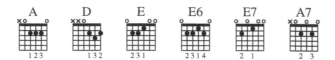

Strum Pattern: 8
Pick Pattern: 8

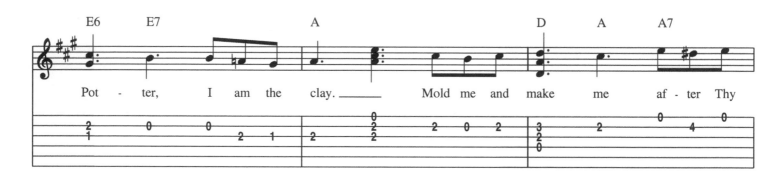

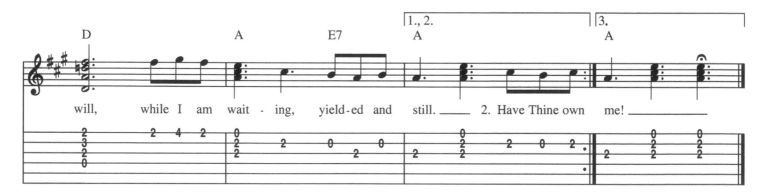

Additional Lyrics

2. Have Thine own way, Lord! Have Thine own way!
   Search me and try me, Master, today!
   Whiter than snow, Lord, wash me just now,
   As in Thy presence humbly I bow.

3. Have Thine own way, Lord! Have Thine own way!
   Hold o'er my being absolute sway!
   Fill with Thy spirit till all shall see
   Christ only, always, living in me!

He's Got the Whole World
in His Hands

African-American Folksong

Strum Pattern: 3, 4
Pick Pattern: 1, 3

1. He's got the whole world _ in His hands, _ He's got the whole world _
2., 3., 4. *See Additional Lyrics*

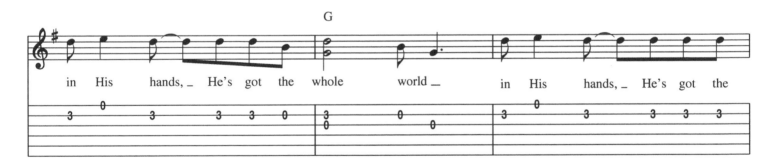

in His hands, _ He's got the whole world _ in His hands, _ He's got the

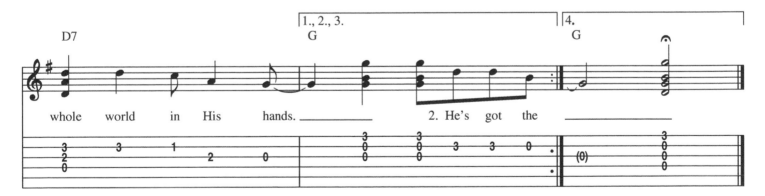

1., 2., 3.

whole world in His hands. _____

4.

2. He's got the _____

Additional Lyrics

2. He's got the wind and the rain in His hands,
He's got the wind and the rain in His hands,
He's got the wind and the rain in His hands,
He's got the whole world in His hands.

3. He's got the tiny little baby in His hands,
He's got the tiny little baby in His hands,
He's got the tiny little baby in His hands,
He's got the whole world in His hands.

4. He's got you and me, brother, in his hands,
He's got you and me, sister, in his hands,
He's got you and me, brother, in his hands,
He's got the whole world in his hands.

Higher Ground

Words by Johnson Oatman, Jr.
Music by Charles H. Gabriel

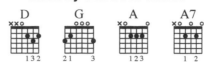

Strum Pattern: 8
Pick Pattern: 8

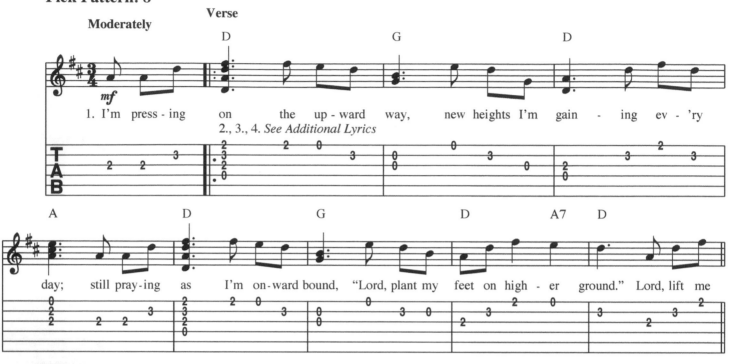

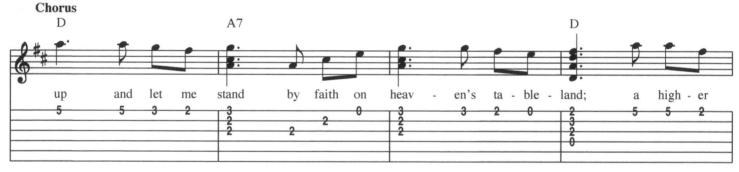

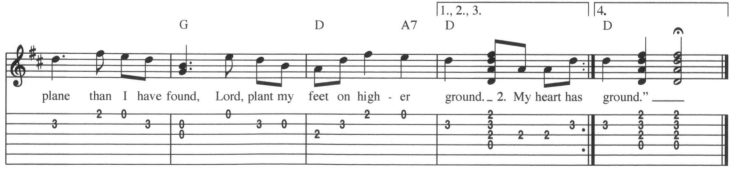

Additional Lyrics

2. My heart has no desire to stay
   Where doubts arise and fears dismay;
   Tho' some may dwell where these abound,
   My prayer, my aim, is higher ground.

3. I want to live above the world,
   Tho' Satan's darts at me are hurled;
   For faith has caught the joyful sound,
   The song of saints on higher ground.

4. I want to scale the utmost height
   And catch a gleam of glory bright;
   But still I'll pray till heav'n I've found,
   "Lord, lead me on to higher ground."

I Feel Like Traveling On

Words by William Hunter
Anonymous Music
Music Arranged by James D. Vaughan

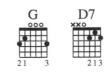

Strum Pattern: 3, 4
Pick Pattern: 1, 3

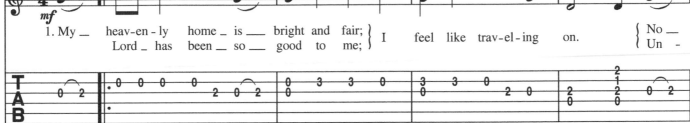

His Eye Is on the Sparrow

Text by Civilla D. Martin
Music by Charles H. Gabriel

Strum Pattern: 8
Pick Pattern: 7

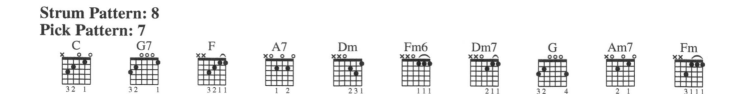

Verse
Warmly

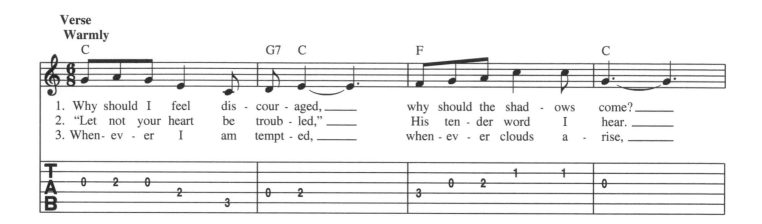

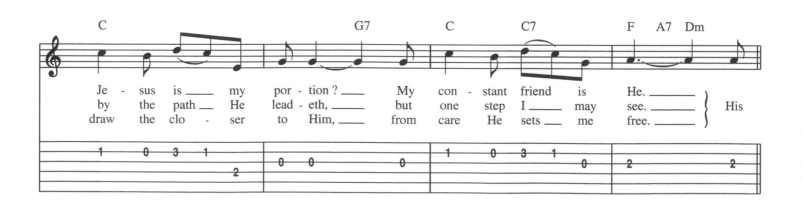

Chorus

eye is on ____ the spar - row, ____ and I know He watch - es me, ____ His

eye is on the spar - row, ____ and I know He watch - es me. ____ I sing be-cause I'm

hap - py, ____ I sing be - cause I'm free; ____ for his eye is on the

spar - row, ____ and I know He watch - es me. ____ me. ____

39

I Have Decided to Follow Jesus

Words by an Indian Prince
Music by Auila Read

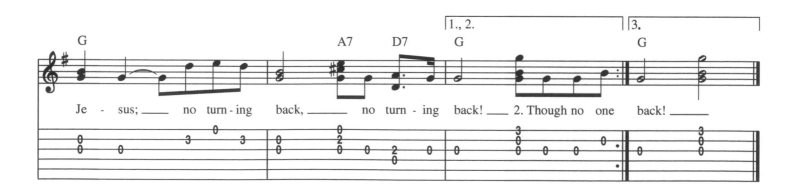

Additional Lyrics

2. Though no one join me, still I will follow.
Though no one join me, still I will follow.
Though no one join me, still I will follow;
No turning back, no turning back!

3. The world behind me, the cross before me;
The world behind me, the cross before me;
The world behind me, the cross before me;
No turning back, no turning back!

I Know Whom I Have Believed

Words by Daniel Whittle
Music by James McGranahan

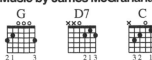

Strum Pattern: 6
Pick Pattern: 6

1. I know not why God's wondrous grace to me He hath made known, nor
2., 3., 4. *See Additional Lyrics*

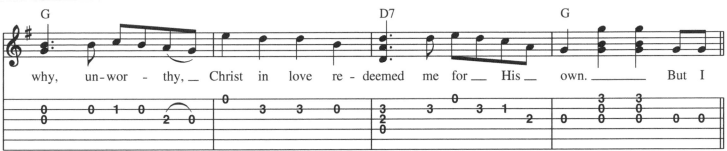

why, unworthy, Christ in love redeemed me for His own. But I

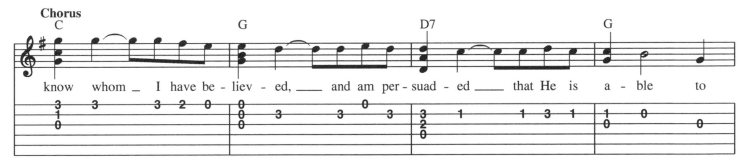

Chorus

know whom I have believed, and am persuaded that He is able to

keep that which I've committed unto Him against that day. 2. I day.

Additional Lyrics

2. I know not how the Spirit moves,
Convincing men of sin,
Revealing Jesus thru the Word,
Creating faith in Him.

3. I know not what of good or ill
May be reserved for me,
Of weary ways or golden days,
Before His face I see.

4. I know not when my Lord may come,
At night of noonday fair,
Nor if I'll walk the vale* with Him,
Or meet Him in the air.

*Valley of Death

I Surrender All

Words by J.W. Van Deventer
Music by W.S. Weeden

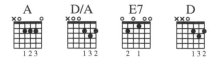

Strum Pattern: 3, 4
Pick Pattern: 2, 4

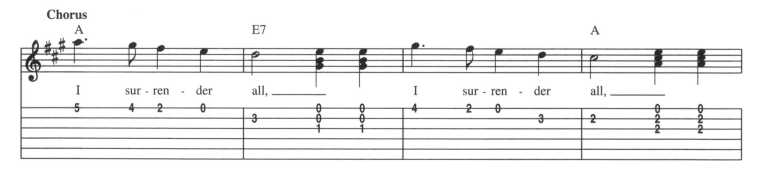

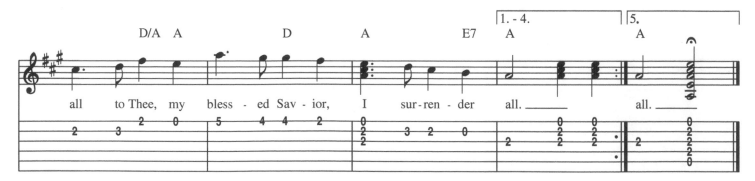

Additional Lyrics

2. All to Jesus I surrender; humbly at His feet I bow,
Worldly pleasures all foresaken; take me, Jesus, take me now.

3. All to Jesus I surrender; make me, Savior, wholly thine;
Let me feel the Holy Spirit, truly know that Thou art mine.

4. All to Jesus I surrender; Lord, I give myself to Thee;
Fill me with Thy love and power; let Thy blessing fall on me.

5. All to Jesus I surrender; now I feel the sacred flame.
O the joy of full salvation! Glory, glory to His name!

I've Got Peace Like a River

Traditional

Strum Pattern: 3
Pick Pattern: 3

Verse
Joyously

1. I've got peace like a riv-er, I've got peace like a
2., 3. *See Additional Lyrics*

riv-er, I've got peace like a riv-er in my soul. _____ I've got

peace like a riv-er, I've got peace like a riv-er, I've got

peace like a riv-er in ___ my soul. (My soul.) 2. I've got soul. (My soul.)

Additional Lyrics

2. I've got love like an ocean,
   I've got love like an ocean,
   I've got love like an ocean in my soul.
   I've got love like an ocean,
   I've got love like an ocean,
   I've got love like an ocean in my soul. (My soul.)

3. I've got joy like a fountain,
   I've got joy like a fountain,
   I've got joy like a fountain in my soul.
   I've got joy like a fountain,
   I've got joy like a fountain,
   I've got joy like a fountain in my soul. (My soul.)

I'm So Glad

Traditional

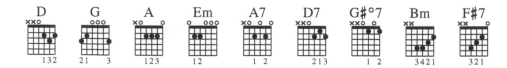

Strum Pattern: 3, 4
Pick Pattern: 1, 3

Chorus
Moderately

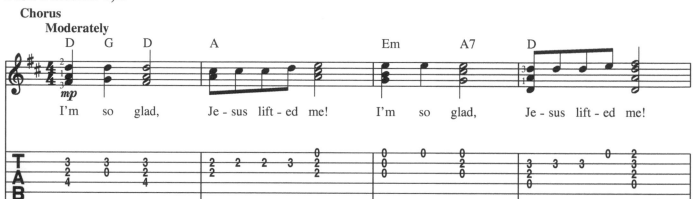

I'm so glad, Je - sus lift - ed me! I'm so glad, Je - sus lift - ed me!

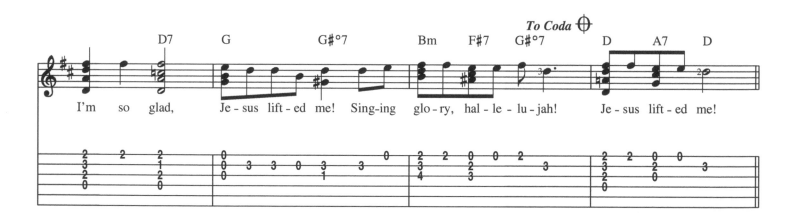

I'm so glad, Je - sus lift - ed me! Sing - ing glo - ry, hal - le - lu - jah! Je - sus lift - ed me!

To Coda ⊕

Verse

1. I was sink - ing down, Je - sus lift - ed me! I was sink - ing down,
2. *See Additional Lyrics*

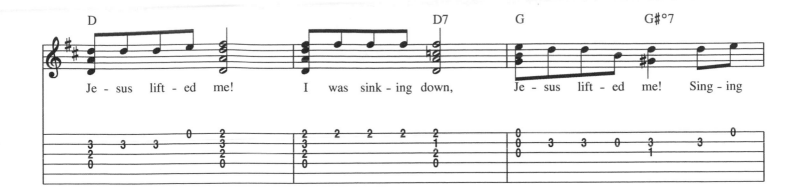

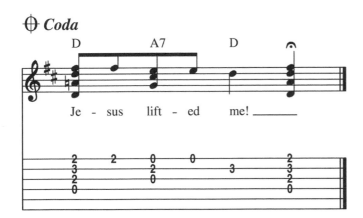

Additional Lyrics

2. Satan had me bound, Jesus lifted me!
Satan had me bound, Jesus lifted me!
Satan had me bound, Jesus lifted me!
Singing glory, hallelujah! Jesus lifted me!

In the Garden

Words and Music by C. Austin Miles

Strum Pattern: 8, 9
Pick Pattern: 8, 9

me, and He tells me I am His own,

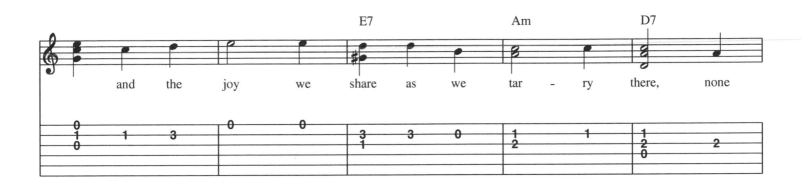

and the joy we share as we tar - ry there, none

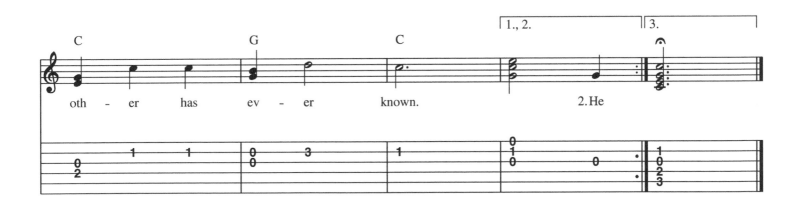

oth - er has ev - er known. 2. He

Additional Lyrics

2. He speaks, and the sound of His voice
   Is so sweet the birds hush their singing,
   And the melody that He gave to me
   Within my heart is ringing.

3. I'd stay in the garden with Him,
   Though the night around me be falling.
   But He bids me go through the voice of woe;
   His voice to me is calling.

Jesus Paid It All

Words and Music by H.M. Hall and John T. Grape

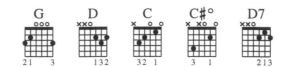

Strum Pattern: 8
Pick Pattern: 8

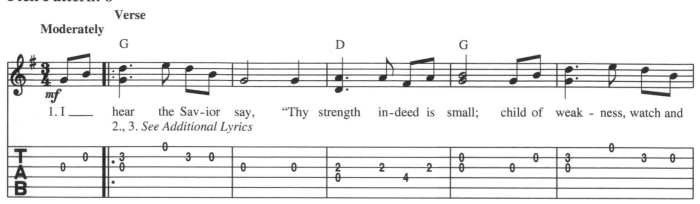

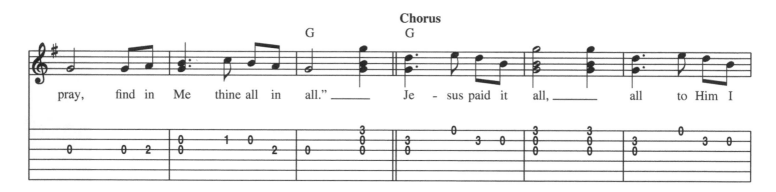

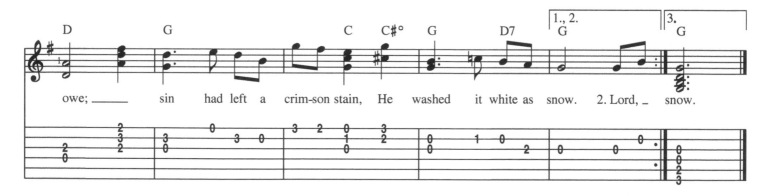

1. I ____ hear the Sav-ior say, "Thy strength in-deed is small; child of weak - ness, watch and pray, find in Me thine all in all." ____ Je - sus paid it all, ____ all to Him I owe; ____ sin had left a crim-son stain, He washed it white as snow. 2. Lord, _ snow.

2., 3. *See Additional Lyrics*

Additional Lyrics

2. Lord, now indeed I find
   Thy pow'r and Thine alone,
   Can change the leper's spots,
   And melt the heart of stone.

3. And when before the throne
   I stand in Him complete,
   I'll lay my trophies down,
   All down at Jesus' feet.

Just a Closer Walk With Thee

Traditional
Arranged by Kenneth Morris

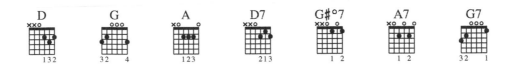

Strum Pattern: 3, 4
Pick Pattern: 3, 4

Intro
Country Swing

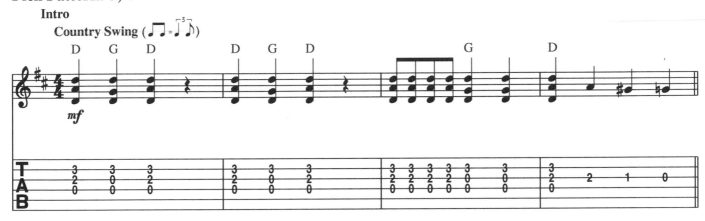

Verse

1. I _____ am weak but Thou art strong. _____
2. *See Additional Lyrics*

Je - sus keep _ me _ from all wrong. _____

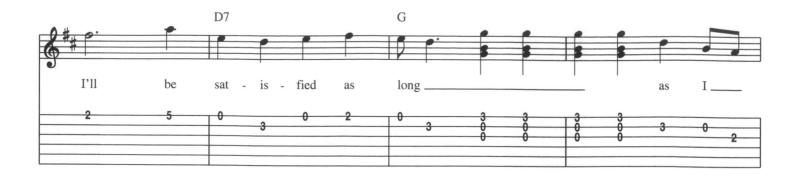

I'll be sat - is - fied as long _____ as I ____

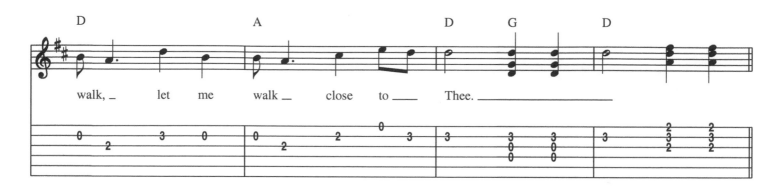

walk, _ let me walk _ close to ____ Thee. _____

Chorus

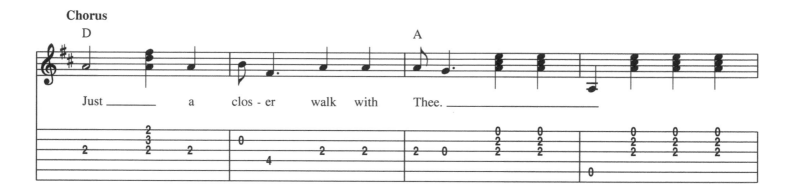

Just _____ a clos - er walk with Thee. _____

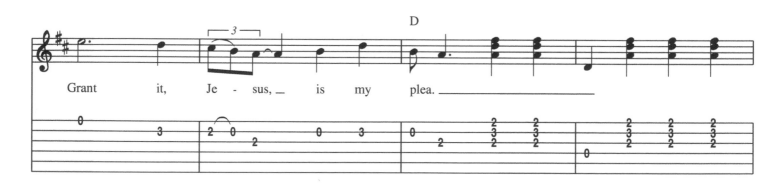

Grant it, Je - sus, _ is my plea. _____

To Coda ⊕

Dai - ly walk - ing close to Thee. _____ Let it be, _

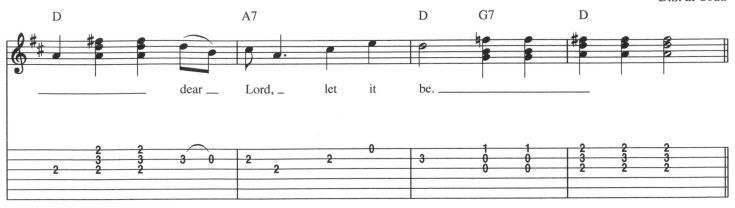

dear Lord, let it be.

⊕ *Coda*

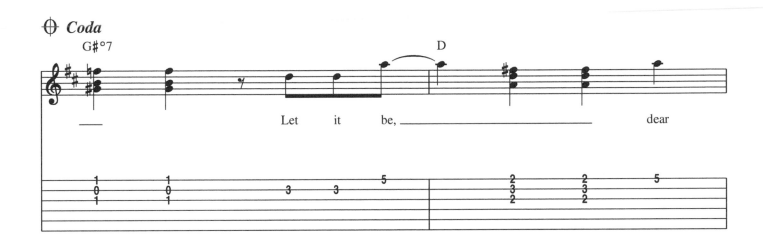

Let it be, dear

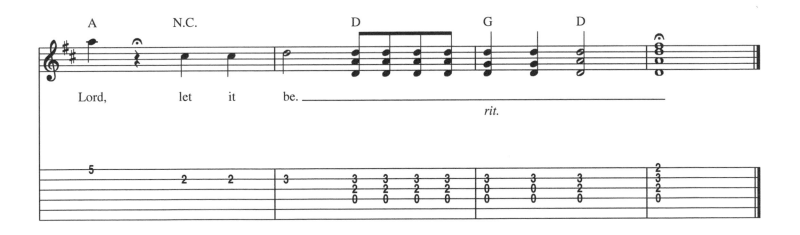

Lord, let it be.

rit.

Additional Lyrics

2. When my feeble life is o'er,
   Time for me will be no more.
   Guide me gently safely o'er
   To Thy Kingdom shore to Thy shore.

Just Over in the Gloryland

Words and Music by J.W. Acuff and Emmett Dean

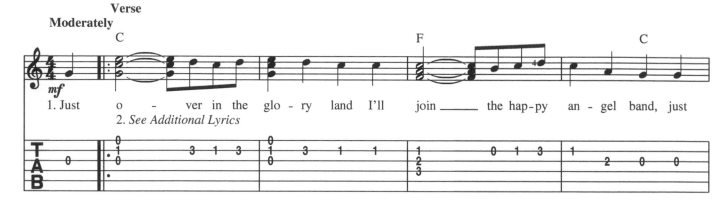

Strum Pattern: 3, 4
Pick Pattern: 1, 3

Verse
Moderately

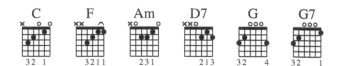

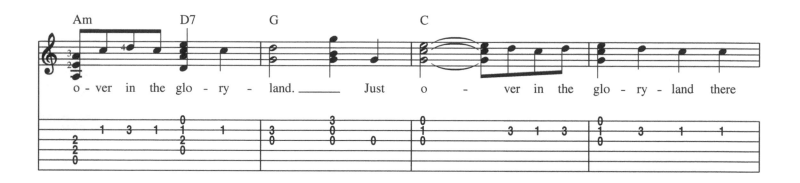

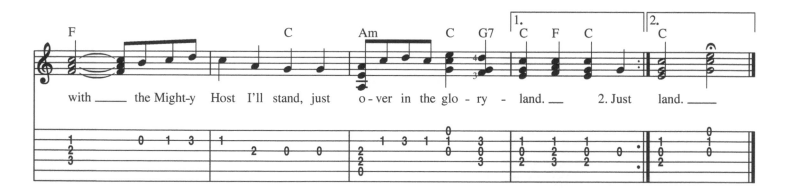

Additional Lyrics

2. Just over, over in the gloryland
   I'll join, yes, join the happy angel band,
   Just over in the gloryland.
   Just over, over in the gloryland,
   There with, yes, with the Mighty Host I'll stand,
   Just over in the gloryland.

Little Is Much When God Is in It

Words by Mrs. F.W. Suffield and Dwight Brock
Music by Mrs. F.W. Suffield

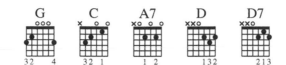

Strum Pattern: 8
Pick Pattern: 8

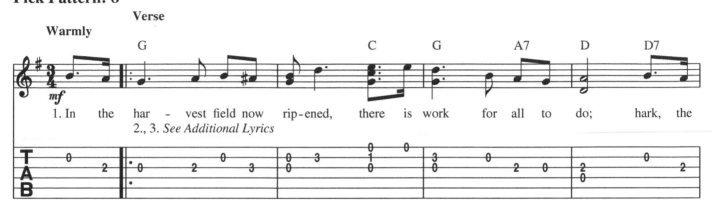

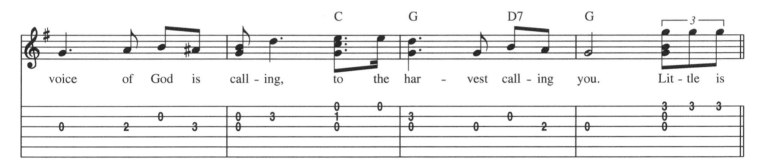

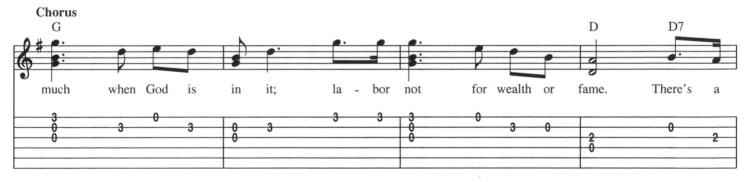

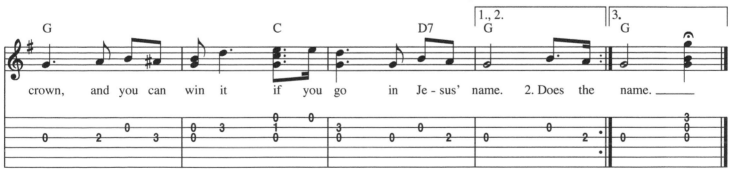

Additional Lyrics

2. Does the place you're called to labor
   Seem so small and little known?
   It is great if God is in it,
   And He'll not forget His own.

3. When the conflict here is ended
   And our race on earth is run;
   He will say, if we are faithful,
   "Welcome home, my child, well done."

Leaning on the Everlasting Arms

Words by Elisha A. Hoffman
Music by Anthony J. Showalter

Strum Pattern: 1
Pick Pattern: 2

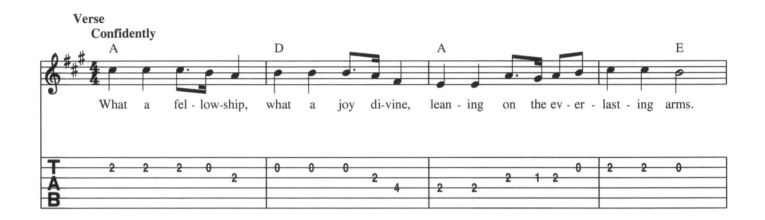

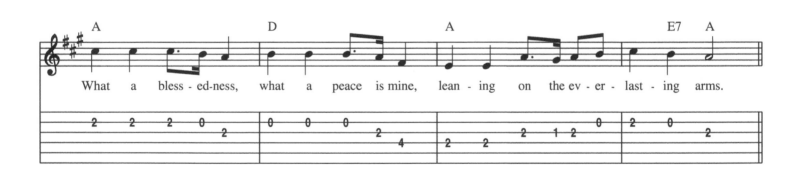

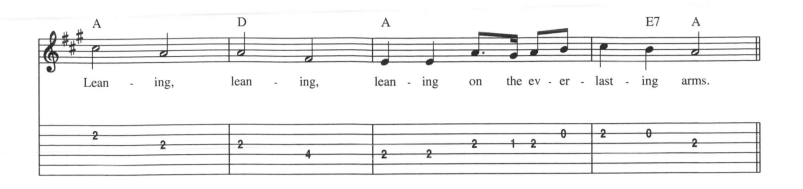

Lean - ing, lean - ing, lean - ing on the ev - er - last - ing arms.

Verse

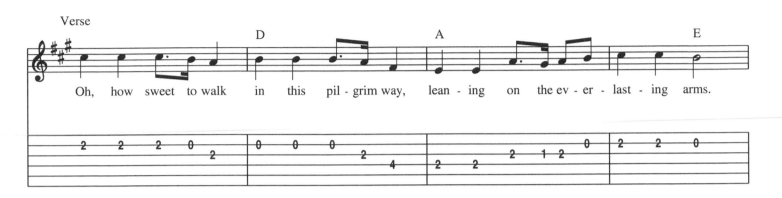

Oh, how sweet to walk in this pil - grim way, lean - ing on the ev - er - last - ing arms.

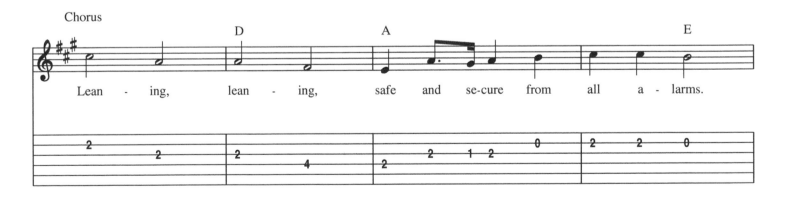

Oh, how bright the path grows from day to day, lean - ing on the ev - er - last - ing arms.

Chorus

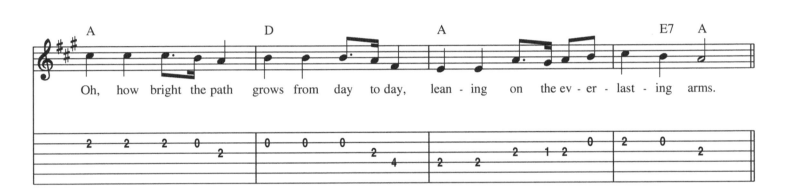

Lean - ing, lean - ing, safe and se-cure from all a - larms.

Lean - ing, lean - ing, lean - ing on the ev - er last - ing arms.

Life's Railway to Heaven

Words and Music by M.E. Abbey

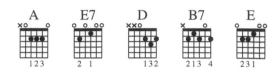

Strum Pattern: 8
Pick Pattern: 8

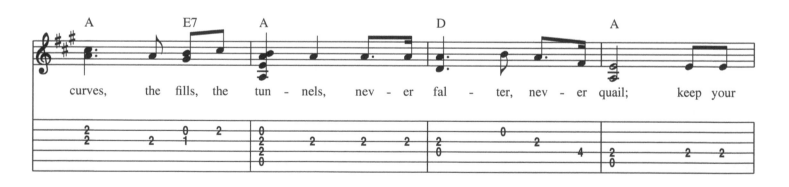

Chorus

Sav - ior, Thou wilt guide us, till we reach the bliss - ful shore, where the

an - gels wait to join us in Thy praise for - ev - er - more. 2. You will more. _____

Additional Lyrics

2. You will roll up grades of trial,
   You will cross the bridge of strife;
   See that Christ is your conductor
   On this lightning train of life.
   Always mindful of obstruction,
   Do your duty, never fail;
   Keep your hand upon the throttle
   And your eye upon the rail.

3. You will often find obstructions,
   Look for storms of wind and rain;
   On a fill or curve or trestle,
   They will almost ditch your train.
   Put your trust alone in Jesus,
   Never falter, never fail;
   Keep your hand upon the throttle
   And your eye upon the rail.

4. As you roll across the trestle,
   Spanning Jordan's swelling tide;
   You behold the Union Depot
   Into which your train will glide.
   There you'll meet the Sup'rintendent,
   God the Father, God the Son,
   With the hearty, joyous plaudit,
   "Weary pilgrim, welcome home."

The Lily of the Valley

Words by Charles W. Fry
Music by William S. Hays

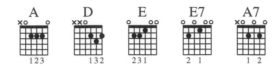

Strum Pattern: 3, 4
Pick Pattern: 1, 3

Verse
Moderately Fast

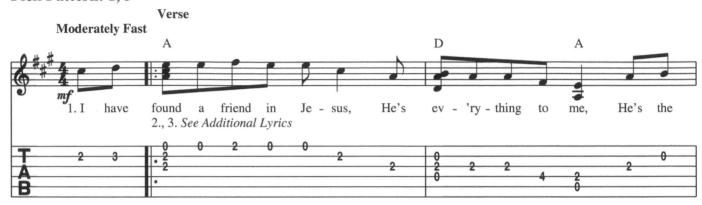

1. I have found a friend in Je-sus, He's ev-'ry-thing to me, He's the
2., 3. *See Additional Lyrics*

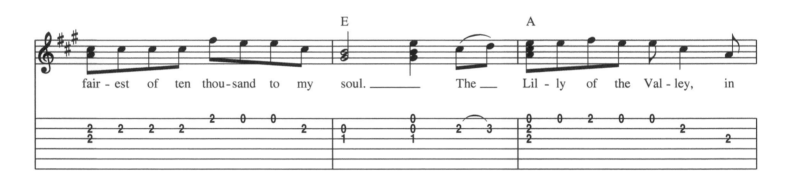

fair-est of ten thou-sand to my soul. _____ The __ Lil-ly of the Val-ley, in

Him a-lone I see all I need to cleanse and make me ful-ly

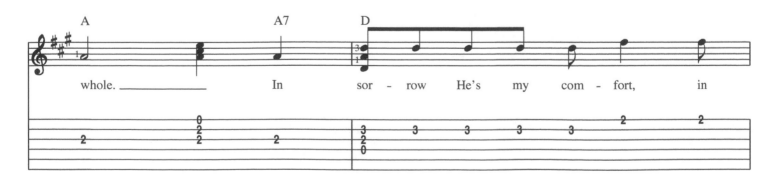

whole. _____ In sor-row He's my com-fort, in

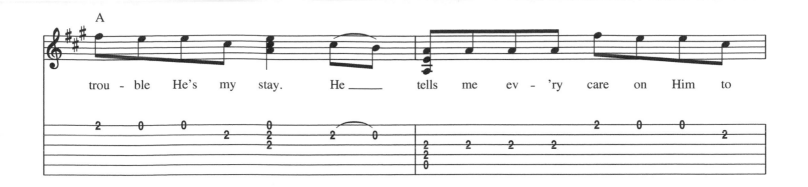

trou - ble He's my stay. He _____ tells me ev - 'ry care on Him to

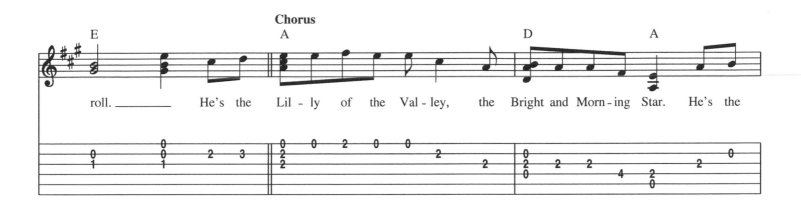

Chorus

roll. _____ He's the Lil - ly of the Val - ley, the Bright and Morn - ing Star. He's the

fair - est of ten thou - sand to my soul. _____ 2. He _____ soul. _____

Additional Lyrics

2. He all my griefs has taken and all my sorrows borne,
   In temptation He's my strong and mighty tow'r.
   I have all for Him forsaken and all my idols torn
   From my heart, and now He keeps me by His pow'r.
   Though all the world forsake me and Satan tempt me sore,
   Through Jesus I shall safely reach the goal.

3. He will never, never leave me nor yet forsake me here,
   While I live by faith and do His blessed will.
   A wall of fire about me, I've nothing now to fear;
   Will His manna He my hungry soul shall fill.
   Then sweeping up to glory I'll see His blessed face
   Where rivers of delight shall ever roll.

The Love of God

Words and Music by Frederick M. Lehman

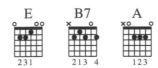

Strum Pattern: 8
Pick Pattern: 8

1. The love of God is great - er far ____ than tongue or pen can ev - er

2., 3. *See Additional Lyrics*

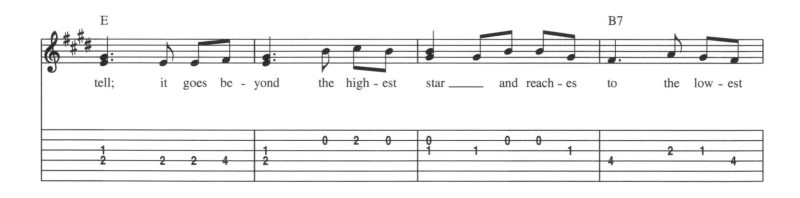

tell; it goes be - yond the high - est star ____ and reach - es to the low - est

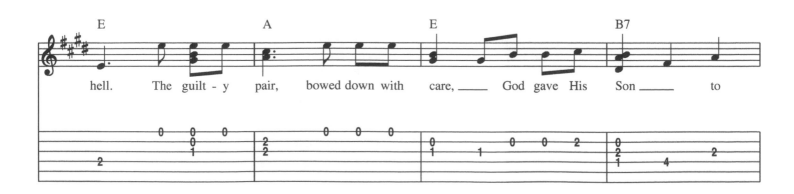

hell. The guilt - y pair, bowed down with care, ____ God gave His Son ____ to

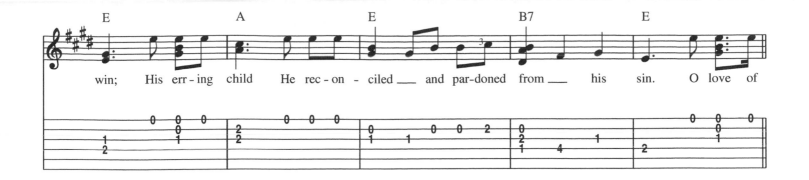

win; His err-ing child He rec-on-ciled ___ and par-doned from ___ his sin. O love of

Chorus

God, how rich and pure! ___ How mea-sure-less ___ and strong! It shall for-

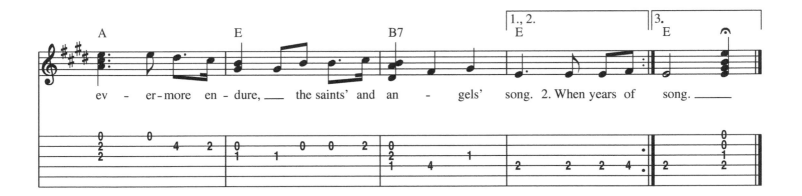

ev - er-more en-dure, ___ the saints' and an - gels' song. 2. When years of song. ___

Additional Lyrics

2. When years of time shall pass away
   And earthly thrones and kingdoms fall,
   When men, who here refuse to pray,
   On rocks and hills and mountains call;
   God's love so sure shall still endure,
   All measureless and strong.
   Redeeming grace to Adam's race,
   The saints' and angels' song.

3. Could we with ink the ocean fill,
   And were the skies of parchment made,
   Were ev'ry stalk on earth a quill,
   And ev'ry man a scribe by trade;
   To write the love of God above
   Would drain the ocean dry;
   Nor could the scroll contain the whole,
   Though stretched from sky to sky.

Near the Cross

Words by Fanny Crosby
Music by William H. Doane

Strum Pattern: 8
Pick Pattern: 8

Verse
Moderately

1. Je - sus, keep me near the cross, there a pre - cious foun - tain,
2., 3., 4. *See Additional Lyrics*

free to all, a heal - ing stream, flows from Cal - v'ry's moun - tain.

Chorus

In the cross, in the cross be my glo - ry ev - er,

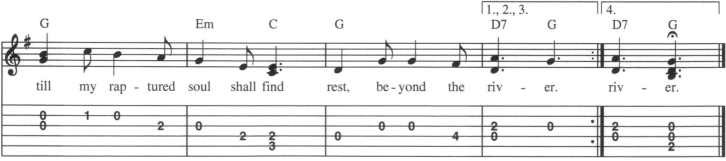

till my rap - tured soul shall find rest, be - yond the riv - er. riv - er.

Additional Lyrics

2. Near the cross, a trembling soul,
   Love and mercy found me.
   There the bright and morning star
   Sheds its beams around me.

3. Near the cross! Oh Lamb of God,
   Bring its scenes before me.
   Help my walk from day to day,
   With its shadows o'er me.

4. Near the cross I'll watch and wait,
   Hoping, trusting ever,
   Till I reach the golden strand
   Just beyond the river.

Nothing But the Blood

Words and Music by Robert Lowry

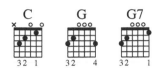

Strum Pattern: 3, 4
Pick Pattern: 1, 3

Verse
Moderately

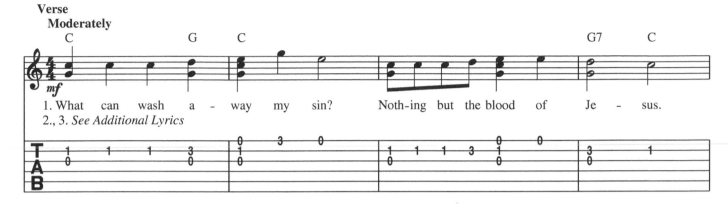

1. What can wash a - way my sin? Noth-ing but the blood of Je - sus.
2., 3. *See Additional Lyrics*

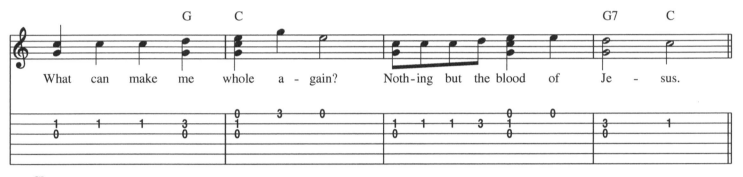

What can make me whole a - gain? Noth-ing but the blood of Je - sus.

Chorus

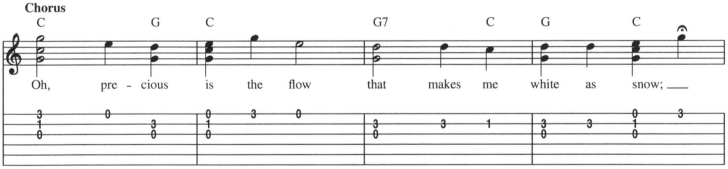

Oh, pre - cious is the flow that makes me white as snow; ___

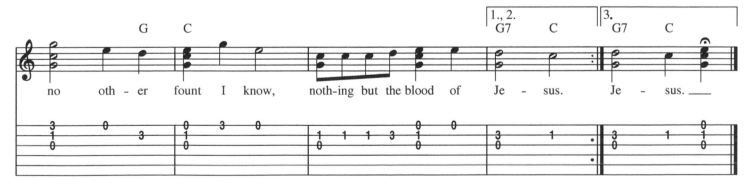

no oth - er fount I know, noth-ing but the blood of Je - sus. Je - sus. ___

Additional Lyrics

2. For my pardon this I see
Nothing but the blood of Jesus;
For my cleansing this my plea:
Nothing but the blood of Jesus.

3. Nothing can for sin atone,
Nothing but the blood of Jesus;
Naught of good that I have done;
Nothing but the blood of Jesus.

A New Name in Glory

Words and Music by C. Austin Miles

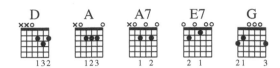

Strum Pattern: 3, 4
Pick Pattern: 1, 3

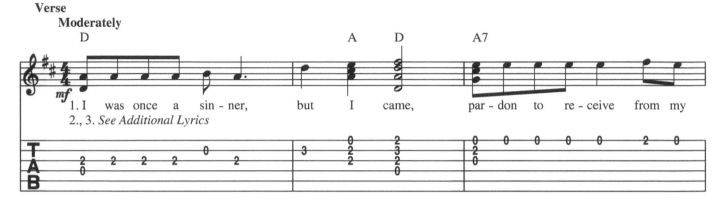

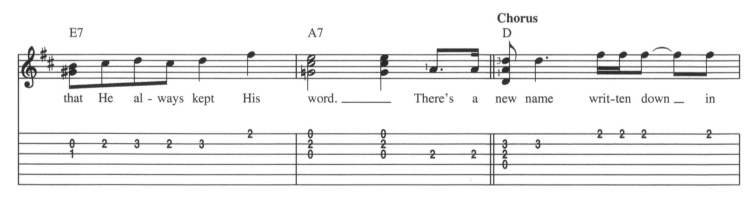

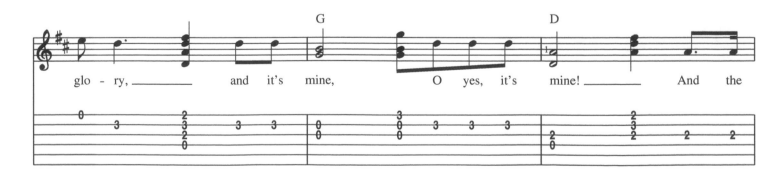

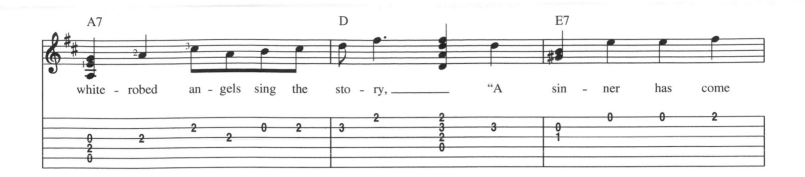

white - robed an - gels sing the sto - ry, _____ "A sin - ner has come

home." For there's a new name writ-ten down __ in glo - ry, _____ and it's

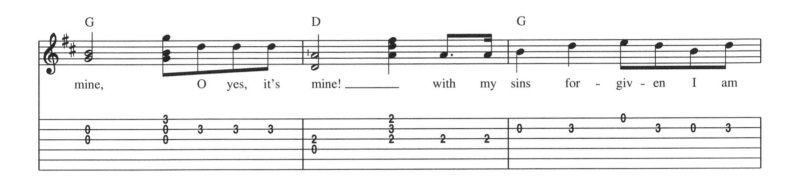

mine, O yes, it's mine! _____ with my sins for - giv - en I am

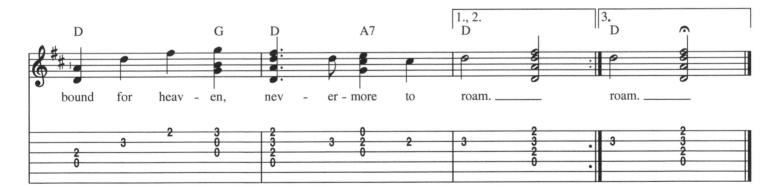

bound for heav - en, nev - er - more to roam. _____ roam. _____

Additional Lyrics

2. I was humbly kneeling at the cross,
   Fearing naught but God's angry frown,
   When the heavens opened and I saw
   That my name was written down.

3. In the Book 'tis written, "Saved by grace."
   O, the joy that came to my soul!
   Now I am forgiven, and I know
   By the blood I am made whole.

The Old Landmark

Traditional

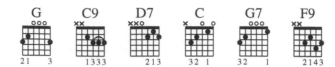

Strum Pattern: 3, 4
Pick Pattern: 1, 3

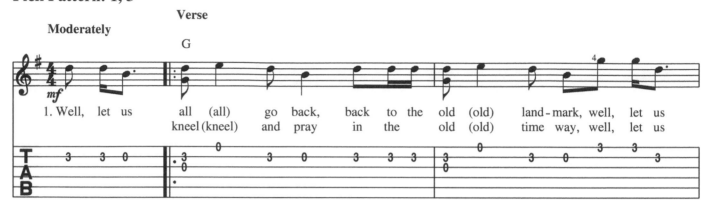

1. Well, let us all (all) go back, back to the old (old) land-mark, well, let us
kneel (kneel) and pray in the old (old) time way, well, let us

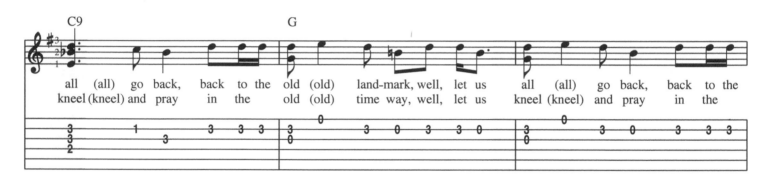

all (all) go back, back to the old (old) land-mark, well, let us all (all) go back, back to the
kneel (kneel) and pray in the old (old) time way, well, let us kneel (kneel) and pray in the

1.

old (old) land-mark, let us stay in the ser-vice of the Lord. _____ 2. Well, let us

2.

old (old) time way. He will (hear us) and be (near us,) we'll be (giv-en) bread from (heav-en,) tell the

Chorus

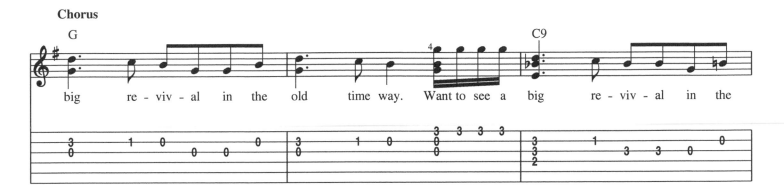

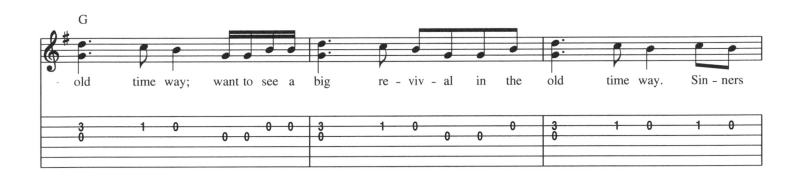

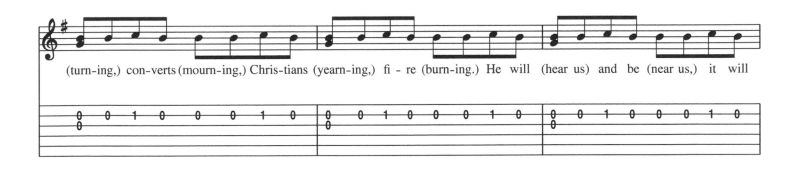

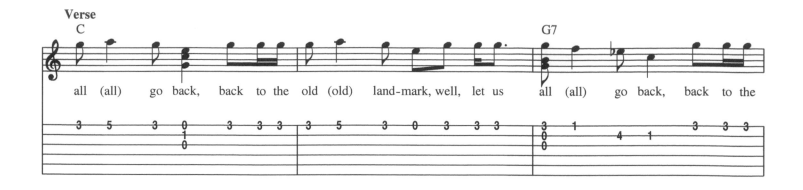

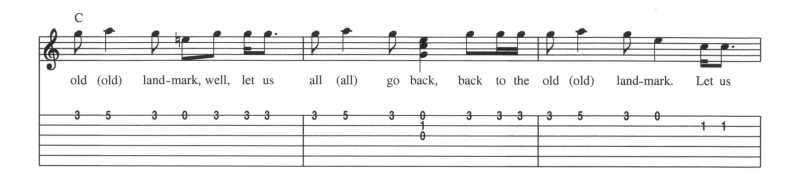

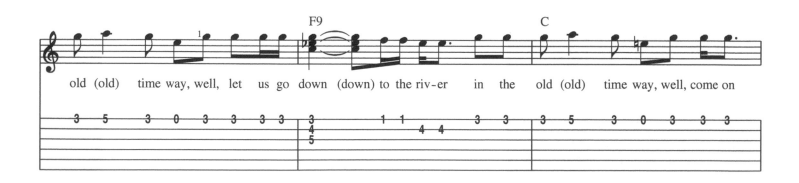

(daugh-ters) bur-ied in (wa-ters) com-in' up a (shout-ing,) no-bod-y (doubt-ing,) He will

(hear us) and be (near us.) We'll be (giv-en) bread from (heav-en,) tell the (sto-ry) of His (glo-ry,) it will

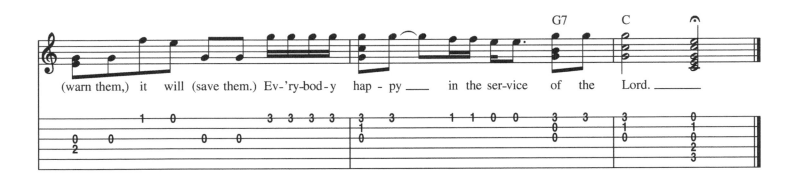

(warn them,) it will (save them.) Ev-'ry-bod-y hap-py ____ in the ser-vice of the Lord. ____

The Old Rugged Cross

Words and Music by Rev. George Bennard

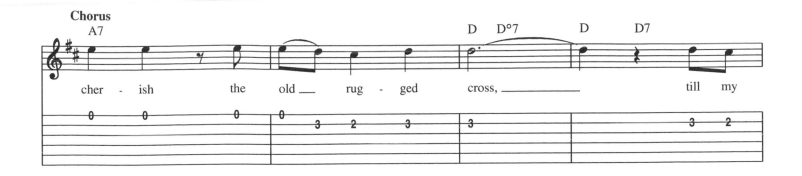

Chorus

cher - ish   the   old __ rug - ged   cross, _____   till my

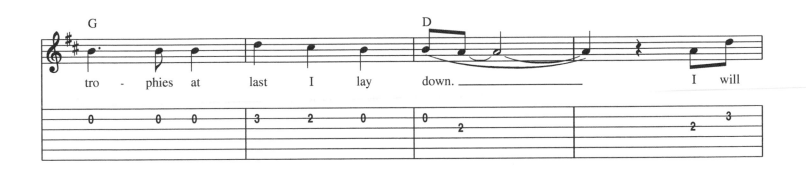

tro - phies   at   last   I   lay   down. _____   I will

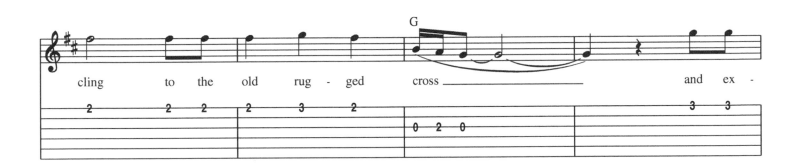

cling   to   the   old   rug - ged   cross _____   and ex -

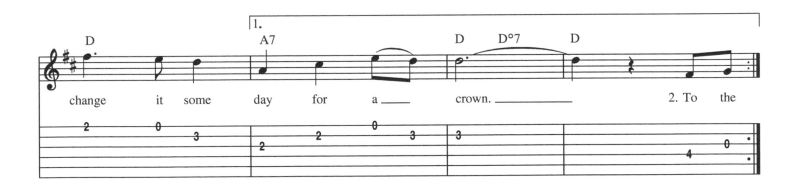

change   it   some   day   for   a __   crown. _____   2. To the

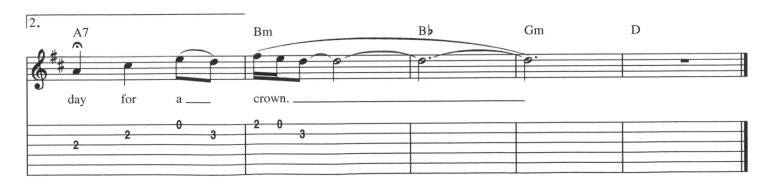

day   for   a __   crown. _____

On Jordan's Stormy Banks

Words by Samuel Stennett
American Folk Hymn
Arranged by Rigdon M. McIntosh

Strum Pattern: 3, 4
Pick Pattern: 1, 3

Additional Lyrics

2. All o'er those wide extended plains
Shines one eternal day;
There God the Son forever reigns
And scatters night away.

3. No chilling winds nor pois'nous breath
Can reach that healthful shore;
Sickness and sorrow, pain and death
Are felt and feared no more.

4. When shall I reach that happy place,
And be forever blest?
When shall I see my Father's face,
And in His bosom rest?

Rock of Ages

Text by Augustus M. Toplady
Music by Thomas Hastings

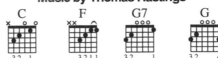

Strum Pattern: 8
Pick Pattern: 8

Additional Lyrics

2. Could my tears forever flow,
   Could my zeal no languor know?
   These for sin could not atone,
   Thou must save and Thou alone.
   I my hand no price I bring,
   Simply to Thy cross I cling.

3. While I draw this fleeting breath,
   When my eyes shall close in death.
   When I rise to worlds unknown,
   And behold Thee on Thy throne.
   Rock of ages cleft for me,
   Let me hide myself in Thee.

Precious Memories

Words and Music by J.B.F. Wright

Strum Pattern: 10
Pick Pattern: 10

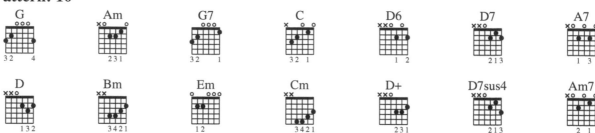

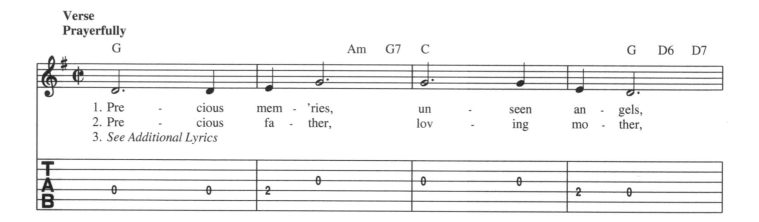

Verse
Prayerfully

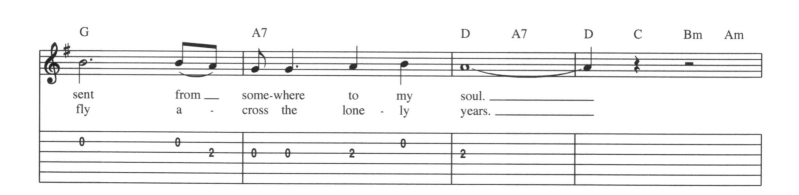

1. Pre - cious mem - 'ries, un - seen an - gels,
2. Pre - cious fa - ther, lov - ing mo - ther,
3. *See Additional Lyrics*

sent from ___ some-where to my soul. ___
fly a - cross the lone - ly years. ___

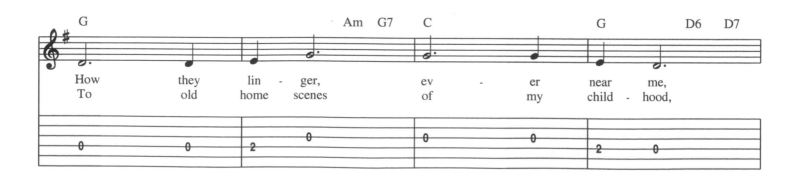

How they lin - ger, ev - er near me,
To old home scenes of my child - hood,

3. As I travel on life's pathway, I know what life shall hold.
As I wander hopes grow fonder. Precious mem'ries flood my soul.

Send the Light

Words and Music by Charles Gabriel

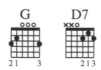

Strum Pattern: 3, 4
Pick Pattern: 1, 3

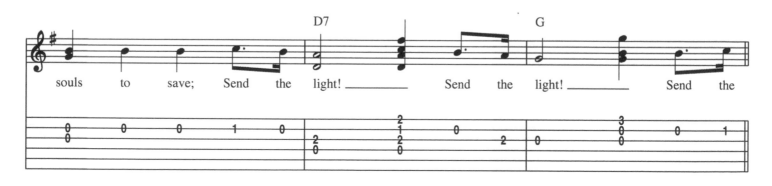

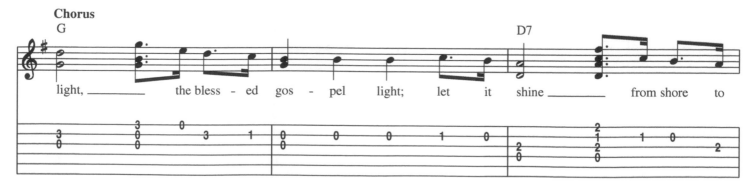

shore! _____ Send the light, _____ the bless - ed gos - pel light; let it

shine _____ for - ev - er - more! _____ 2. We have more! _____

Additional Lyrics

2. We heave heard the Macedonian call today,
   "Send the light! Send the light!"
   And a golden off'ring at the cross we lay;
   Send the light! Send the light!

3. Let us pray that grace may ev'rywhere abound;
   "Send the light! Send the light!"
   And a Christ-like spirit ev'rywhere to be found;
   Send the light! Send the light!

4. Let us not grow weary in the work of love;
   "Send the light! Send the light!"
   Let us gather jewels for a crown above;
   Send the light! Send the light!

Sweet By and By

Words by Sanford Fillmore Bennett
Music by Joseph P. Webster

Strum Pattern: 3
Pick Pattern: 4

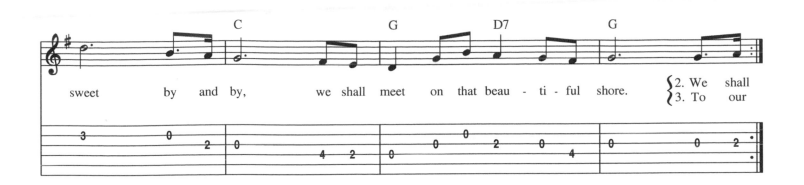

sweet by and by, we shall meet on that beau - ti - ful shore.

2. We shall
3. To our

Verse

boun - ti - ful Fa - ther a - bove we will of - fer our tri - bute of praise for the

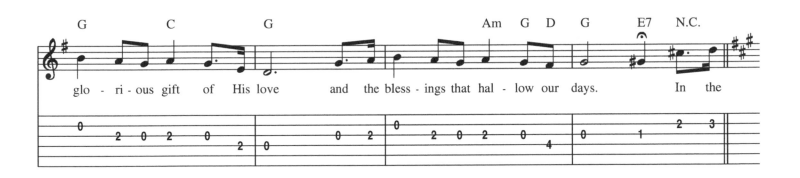

glo - ri - ous gift of His love and the bless - ings that hal - low our days. In the

Chorus

sweet by and by, we shall meet on that beau - ti - ful shore; in the

sweet by and by, we shall meet on that beau - ti - ful shore.

There Is a Fountain

Words by William Cowper
Traditional American Melody Arranged by Lowell Mason

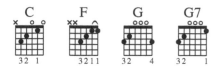

Strum Pattern: 3, 4
Pick Pattern: 1, 3

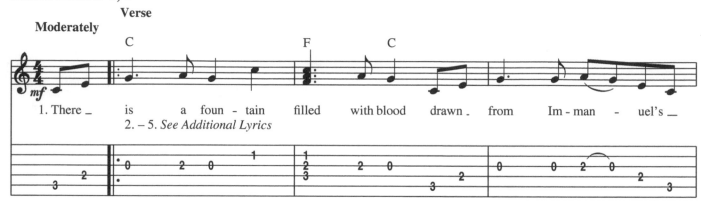

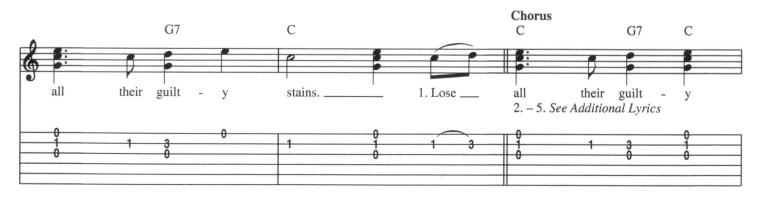

sin - ners, plunged be - neath that flood, lose ___ all their guilt - y

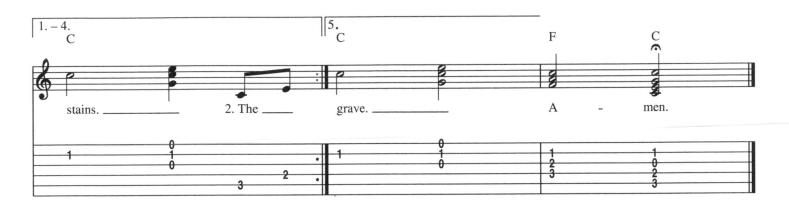

stains. _____ 2. The ___ grave. _____ A - men.

Additional Lyrics

2. The dying thief rejoiced to see
   That fountain in his day;
   And there my I, though vile as he,
   Wash all my sins away.

Chorus 2. Wash all my sins away,
   Wash all my sins away;
   And there may I, though vile as he,
   Wash all my sins away.

3. Dear dying Lamb, Thy precious blood
   Shall never lose its power,
   Till all the ransomed Church of God
   Be saved, to sin no more.

Chorus 3. Be saved, to sin no more,
   Be saved, to sin no more;
   Till all the ransomed Church of God
   Be saved, to sin no more.

4. E'er since by faith, I saw the stream
   Thy flowing wounds supply,
   Redeeming love has been my theme,
   And shall be till I die.

Chorus 4. And shall be till I die,
   And shall be till I die;
   Redeeming love has been my theme,
   And shall be till I die.

5. Then in a nobler, sweeter song,
   I'll sing Thy power to save,
   When this poor lisping, stamm'ring tongue
   Lies silent in the grave.

Chorus 5. Lies silent in the grave,
   Lies silent in the grave;
   When this poor lisping, stamm'ring tongue
   Lies silent in the grave.

There Is Power in the Blood

Words and Music by Lewis E. Jones

Strum Pattern: 3, 4
Pick Pattern: 1, 3

Verse
Brightly

1. Would you be free from the bur-den of sin? There's pow'r in the blood, pow'r in the blood;
2., 3., 4. *See Additional Lyrics*

would you o'er e-vil a vic-to-ry win? There's won-der-ful pow'r in the blood. ___ There is

Chorus

pow'r, pow'r, won-der-work-ing pow'r in the blood ___ of the Lamb; ___ there is

pow'r, pow'r, won-der-work-ing pow'r in the pre-cious blood of the Lamb. ___ Lamb. ___

Additional Lyrics

2. Would you be free from your passion and pride?
   There's pow'r in the blood, pow'r in the blood;
   Come for a cleansing to Calvary's tide;
   There's wonderful pow'r in the blood.

3. Would you be whiter, much whiter than snow?
   There's pow'r in the blood, pow'r in the blood;
   Sin stains are lost in its life giving flow;
   There's wonderful pow'r in the blood.

4. Would you do service for Jesus your King?
   There's pow'r in the blood, pow'r in the blood;
   Would you live daily His praises to sing:
   There's wonderful pow'r in the blood.

Wayfaring Stranger

Southern American Folk Hymn

Strum Pattern: 8
Pick Pattern: 8

Additional Lyrics

2. I'll soon be free from ev'ry trial,
   This form will rest beneath the sod;
   I'll drop the cross of self-denial
   And enter in my home with God.
   I'm going there to see my Savior,
   Who shed for me His precious blood;
   I am just going over Jordan,
   I am just going over home.

Unclouded Day

Words and Music by J.K. Alwood

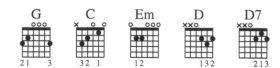

*Strum Pattern: 3, 4
*Pick Pattern: 1, 3

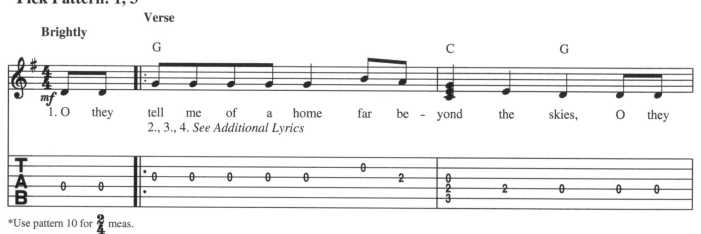

*Use pattern 10 for 2/4 meas.

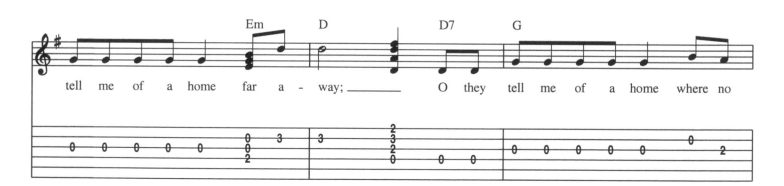

Chorus

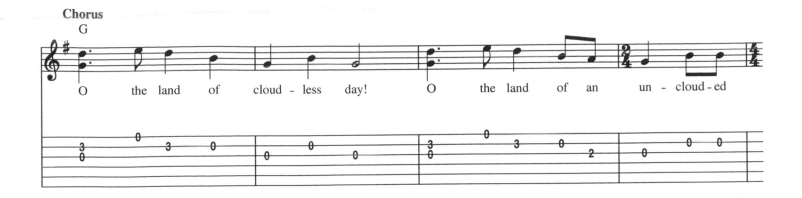

O the land of cloud - less day! O the land of an un - cloud-ed

day! _____ O they tell me of a home where no storm - clouds rise,

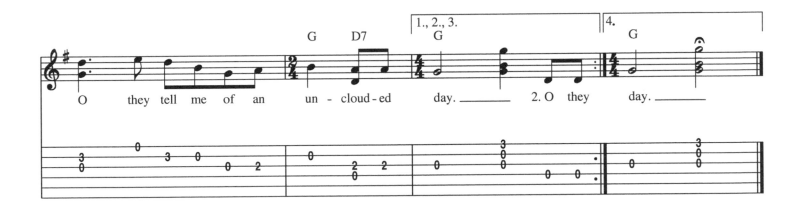

O they tell me of an un - cloud-ed day. _____ 2. O they day. _____

Additional Lyrics

2. O they tell me of a home where my friends have gone,
O they tell me of that land far away,
Where the tree of life in eternal bloom
Sheds its fragrance through the unclouded day.

3. O they tell me of a King in His beauty there,
And they tell me that mine eyes shall behold
Where He sits on the throne that is whiter than snow,
In the city that is made of gold.

4. O they tell me that He smiles on His children there,
And His smile drives their sorrows all away;
And they tell me that no tears ever come again
In that lovely land of unclouded day.

We'll Understand It Better By and By

Words and Music by Charles A. Tindley

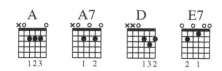

Strum Pattern: 3, 4
Pick Pattern: 1, 3

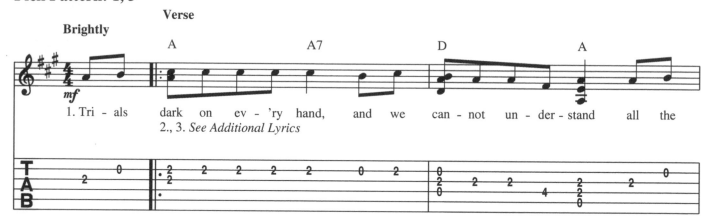

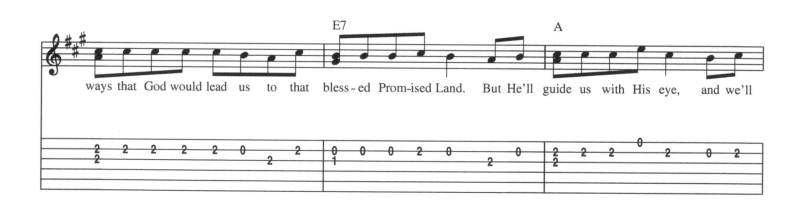

Chorus

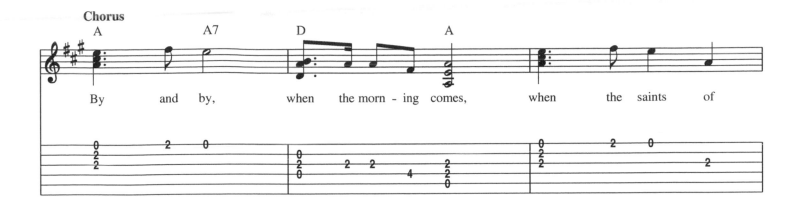

By and by, when the morn - ing comes, when the saints of

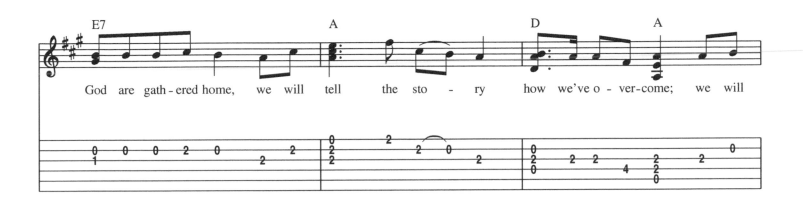

God are gath - ered home, we will tell the sto - ry how we've o - ver-come; we will

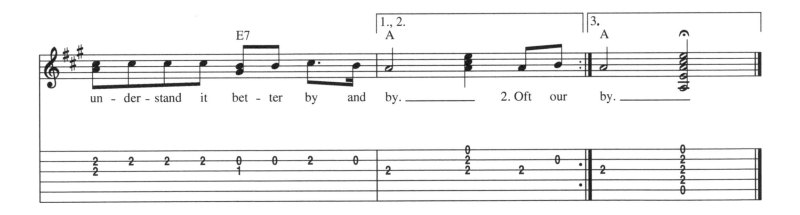

un - der - stand it bet - ter by and by. _____ 2. Oft our by. _____

Additional Lyrics

2. Oft our cherished plans have failed,
Disappointments have prevailed,
And we've wandered in the darkness,
Heavy-hearted and alone.
But we're trusting in the Lord,
And according to His Word,
We will understand it better by and by.

3. Temptations, hidden snares
Often take us unawares,
And our hearts are made to bleed
For some thoughtless word or deed;
And we wonder why the test
When we try to do our best,
But we'll understand it better by and by.

Were You There?

African-American Spiritual

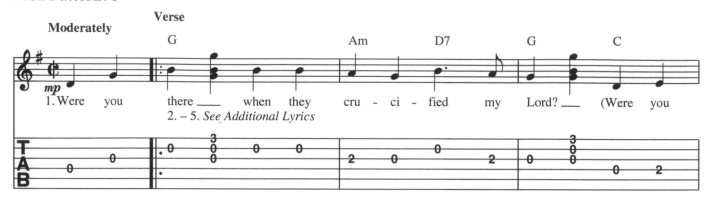

Strum Pattern: 3
Pick Pattern: 3

Moderately

Verse

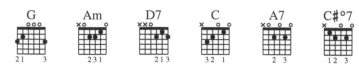

mp

1. Were you there ____ when they cru - ci - fied my Lord? ____ (Were you

2. – 5. *See Additional Lyrics*

there? ____) Were you there ____ when they cru - ci - fied my

Lord? ____ Oh, ____ some - times ____ it

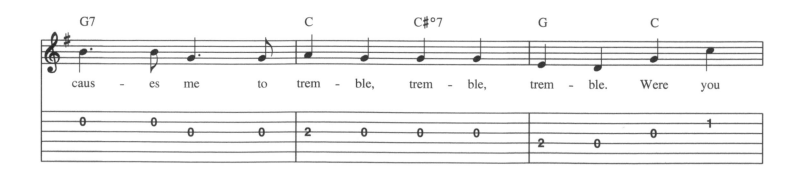

caus - es me to trem - ble, trem - ble, trem - ble. Were you

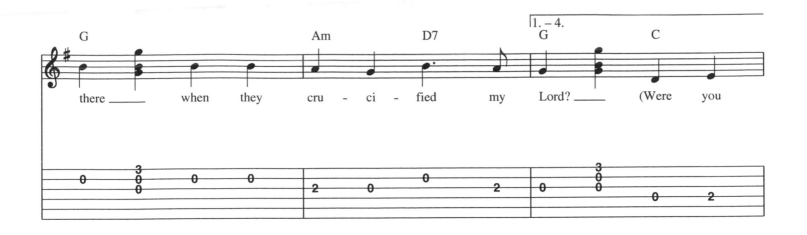

there _____ when they cru - ci - fied my Lord? _____ (Were you

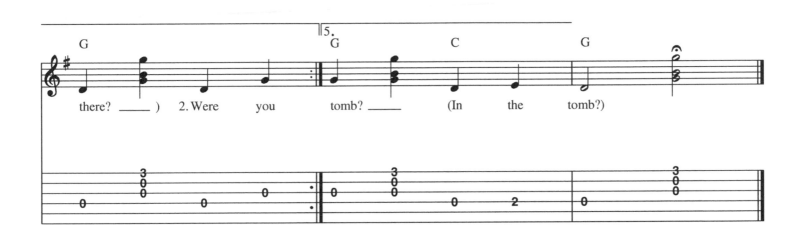

there? _____) 2. Were you tomb? _____ (In the tomb?)

Additional Lyrics

2. Were you there when they nailed Him to the tree? (To the tree?)
   Were you there when they nailed Him to the tree? (To the tree?)
   Oh, sometimes it causes me to tremble, tremble, tremble.
   Were you there when they nailed him to the tree? (To the tree?)

3. Were you there when they pierced Him in the side? (In the side?)
   Were you there when they pierced Him in the side? (In the side?)
   Oh, sometimes it causes me to tremble, tremble, tremble.
   Were you there when they pierced Him in the side? (In the side?)

4. Were you there when the sun refused to shine? (Were you there?)
   Were you there when the sun refused to shine? (Were you there?)
   Oh, sometimes it causes me to tremble, tremble, tremble.
   Were you there when the sun refused to shine? (Were you there?)

5. Were you there when they laid Him in the tomb? (In the tomb?)
   Were you there when they laid Him in the tomb? (In the tomb?)
   Oh, sometimes it causes me to tremble, tremble, tremble.
   Were you there when they laid Him in the tomb? (In the tomb?)

What a Friend We Have in Jesus

Words by Joseph Scriven
Music by Charles C. Converse

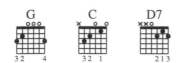

Strum Pattern: 6
Pick Pattern: 4

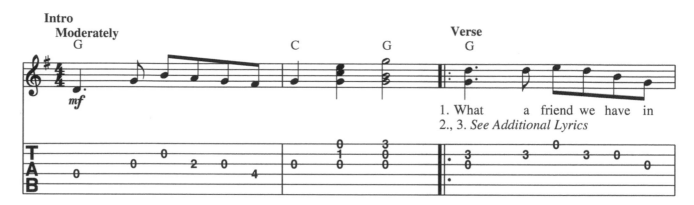

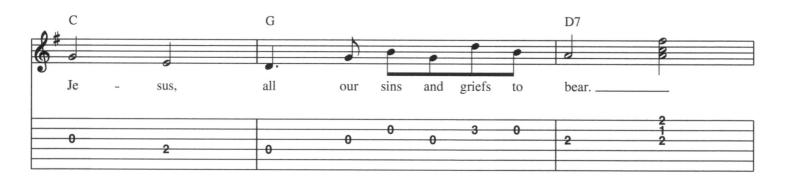

1. What a friend we have in
2., 3. *See Additional Lyrics*

Je - sus, all our sins and griefs to bear. ___

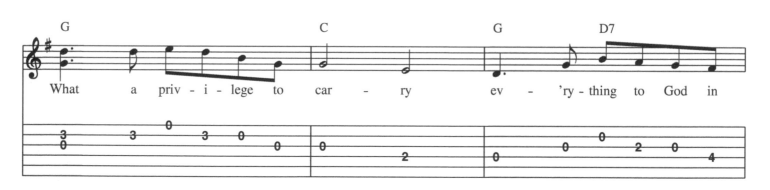

What a priv - i - lege to car - ry ev - 'ry - thing to God in

prayer. ___ Oh, what peace we of - ten for - feit,

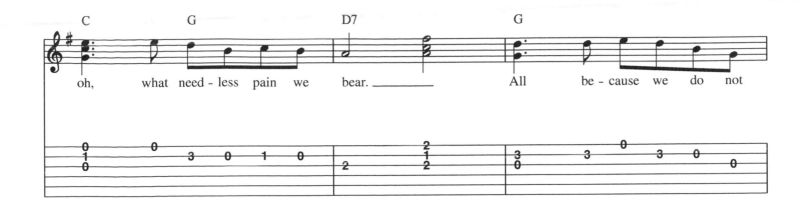

oh,   what need - less pain we bear. _____ All be - cause we do not

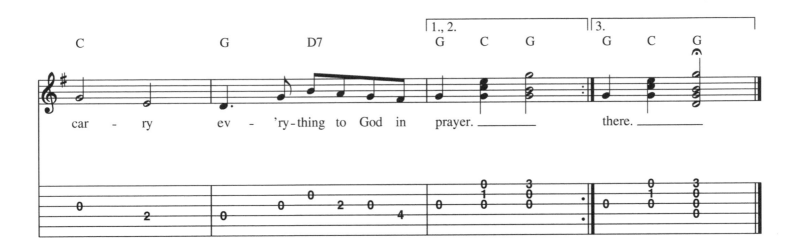

car - ry ev - 'ry-thing to God in prayer. _____ there. _____

Additional Lyrics

2. Have we trials and temptations,
   Is there troubles anywhere?
   We should never be discouraged;
   Take it to the Lord in prayer.
   Can we find a friend so faithful
   Who will all our sorrows share?
   Jesus knows our ev'ry weakness;
   Take it to the Lord in prayer.

3. Are we weak and heavy laden,
   Cumbered with a load of care?
   Precious Savior still our refuge;
   Take it to the Lord in prayer.
   Do thy friends despise, forsake thee?
   Take it to the Lord in prayer.
   In His arms He'll take and shield thee;
   Thou will find a solace there.

When I Can Read My Title Clear

Words by Isaac Watts
Traditional American Melody attributed to Joseph C. Lowry

Strum Pattern: 3, 4
Pick Pattern: 1, 3

Additional Lyrics

2. Should earth, against my soul engage,
   And fiery darts be hurled,
   Then I can smile at Satan's rage
   And face a frowning world.
   And face a frowning world,
   And face a frowning world,
   Then I can smile at Satan's rage
   And face a frowning world.

3. Let cares like a wild deluge come,
   And storms of sorrow fall!
   May I but safely reach my home,
   My God, my heav'n, my all.
   My God, my heav'n, my all,
   My God, my heav'n, my all,
   May I but safely reach my home,
   My God, my heav'n, my all.

4. There shall I bathe my weary soul
   In seas of heav'nly rest,
   And not a wave of trouble roll
   Across my peaceful breast.
   Across my peaceful breast,
   Across my peaceful breast,
   And not a wave of trouble roll
   Across my peaceful breast.

When We All Get to Heaven

Words and Music by E.E. Hewitt and J.G. Wilson

Strum Pattern: 3, 4
Pick Pattern: 1, 3

Verse
Moderately

1. Sing the won-drous love _ of __ Je-sus; sing His mer-cy _ and His grace.
2., 3., 4. *See Additional Lyrics*

In the man-sions, bright and bless-ed, He'll pre-pare for us a place. ___ When we

Chorus

all (When we all.) get to heav-en, what a day of re-joic-ing that will be? ___ When we

all (When we all.) see Je-sus, we'll sing and shout the vic-to-ry. ___ ry. ___

Additional Lyrics

2. While we walk the pilgrim pathway,
   Clouds will overspread the sky;
   But when trav'ling days are over,
   Not a shadow, not a sigh!

3. Let us then be true and faithful,
   Trusting, serving ev'ryday.
   Just one glimpse of Him in glory
   Will the toils of life repay.

4. Onward to the prize before us!
   Soon His beauty we'll behold.
   Soon the pearly gates will open;
   We shall tread the streets of gold.

When the Roll Is Called Up Yonder

Words and Music by James M. Black

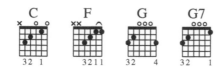

Strum Pattern: 3, 4
Pick Pattern: 1, 3

Verse

Brightly

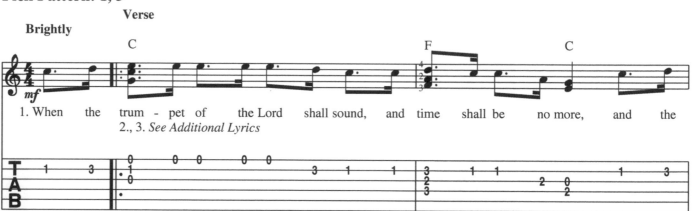

1. When the trum - pet of the Lord shall sound, and time shall be no more, and the
2., 3. *See Additional Lyrics*

morn - ing breaks, e - ter - nal, bright, and fair; _____ when the saved of earth shall gath - er o - ver

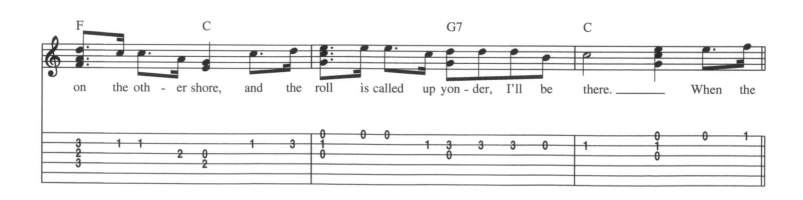

on the oth - er shore, and the roll is called up yon - der, I'll be there. _____ When the

Chorus

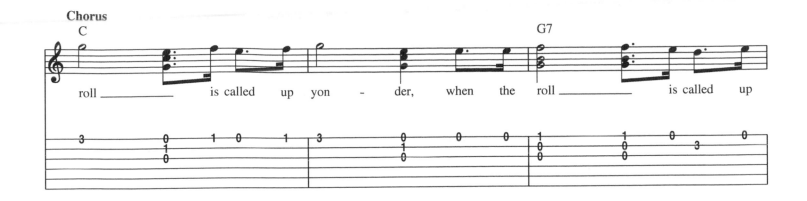

roll _____ is called up yon - der, when the roll _____ is called up

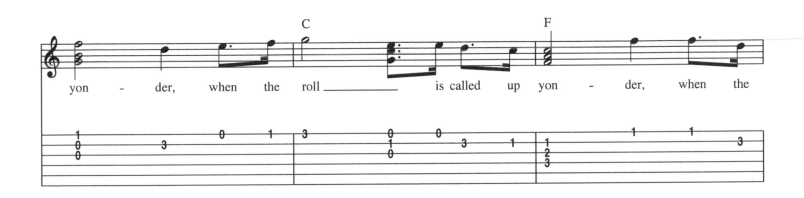

yon - der, when the roll _____ is called up yon - der, when the

roll is called up yon - der, I'll be there. _____ 2. On that there. _____

Additional Lyrics

2. On that bright and cloudless morning when the dead in Christ shall rise,
   And the glory of His resurrection share;
   When His chosen ones shall gather to their home beyond the skies,
   And the roll is called up yonder, I'll be there.

3. Let us labor for the Master from the dawn till setting sun,
   Let us talk of all His wondrous love and care;
   Then when all of life is over and our work on earth is done,
   And the roll is called up yonder, I'll be there.

Whispering Hope

Words and Music by Alice Hawthorne

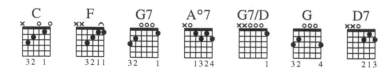

Strum Pattern: 8
Pick Pattern: 8

Verse
Slowly

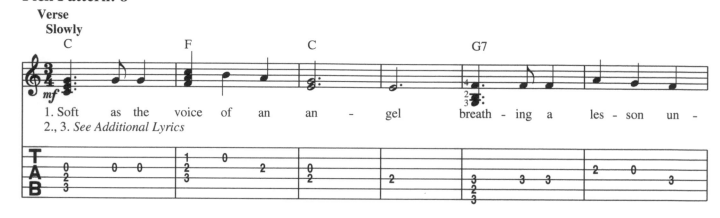

1. Soft as the voice of an an - gel breath - ing a les - son un -
2., 3. *See Additional Lyrics*

heard, _____ hope with a gen - tle per - sua - sion

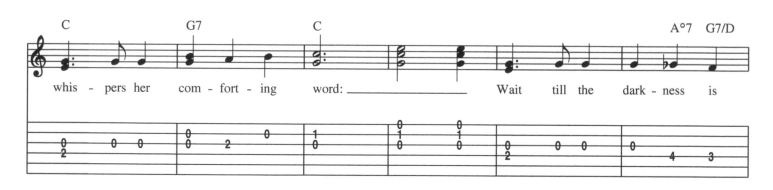

whis - pers her com - fort - ing word: _____ Wait till the dark - ness is

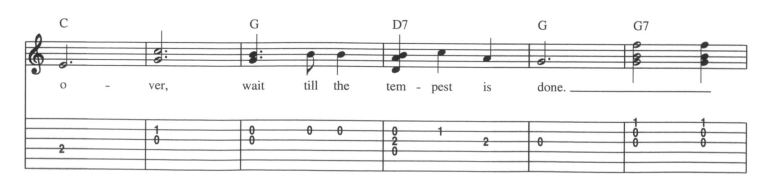

o - ver, wait till the tem - pest is done. _____

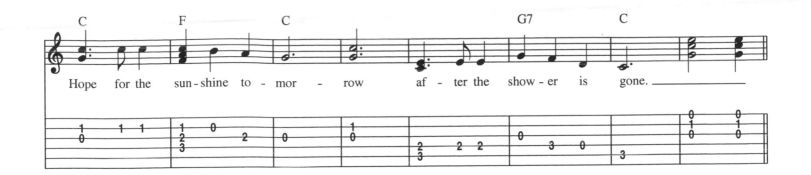

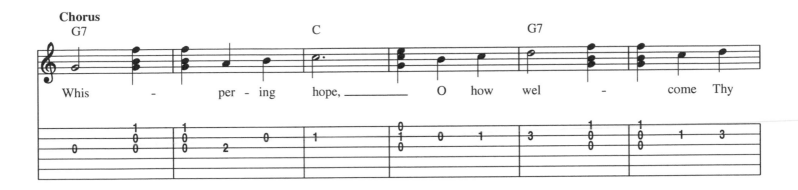

Chorus

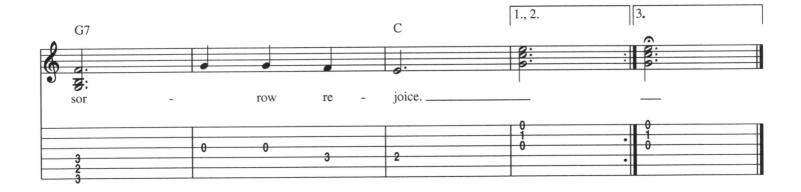

Additional Lyrics

2. If, in the dusk of the twilight,
   Dim be the region afar,
   Will not the deepening darkness
   Brighten the glimmering star?
   Then when the night is upon us,
   Why should the heart sink away?
   When the dark midnight is over,
   Watch for the breaking of day.

3. Hope, as an anchor so steadfast,
   Rends the dark veil for the soul,
   Whither the Master has entered,
   Robbing the grave of its goal.
   Come then, O come, glad fruition,
   Come to my sad, weary heart.
   Come, O Thou blest hope of glory,
   Never, O never depart.

Wonderful Grace of Jesus

Traditional

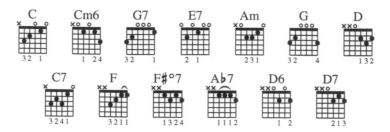

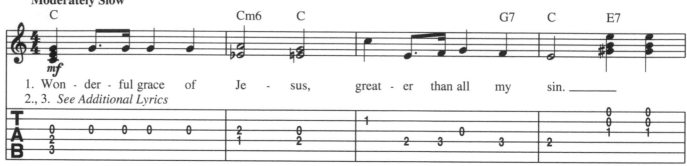

Strum Pattern: 1, 3
Pick Pattern: 2, 4

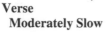

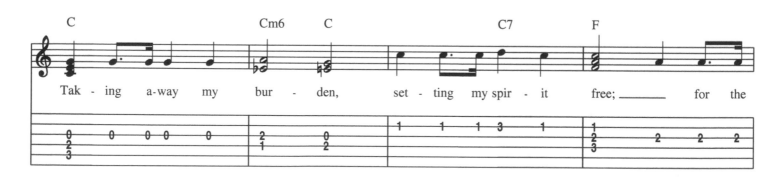

Chorus

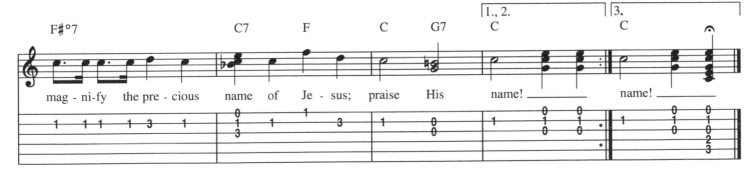

Additional Lyrics

2. Wonderful grace of Jesus, reaching to all the lost.
   By it I have been pardoned, saved to the uttermost.
   Chains have been torn asunder, giving me liberty;
   For the wonderful grace of Jesus reaches me.

3. Wonderful grace of Jesus, reaching the most defiled.
   By its transforming power making Him God's dear child.
   Purchasing peace and heaven for all eternity;
   For the wonderful grace of Jesus reaches me.

Wondrous Love

Southern American Folk Hymn

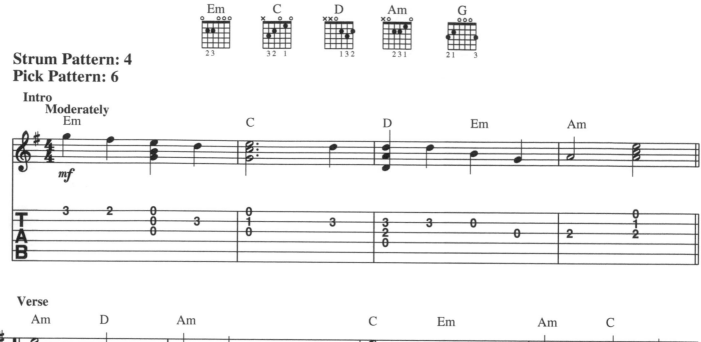

Strum Pattern: 4
Pick Pattern: 6

Intro
Moderately

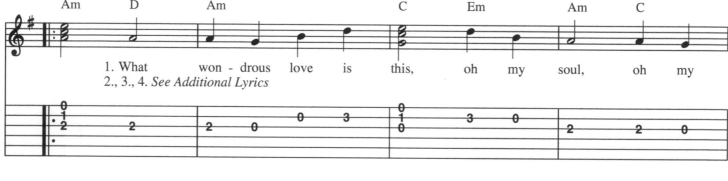

Verse

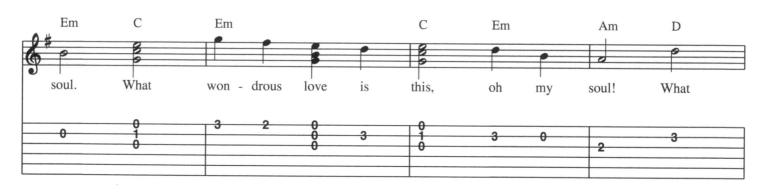

1. What won - drous love is this, oh my soul, oh my
2., 3., 4. *See Additional Lyrics*

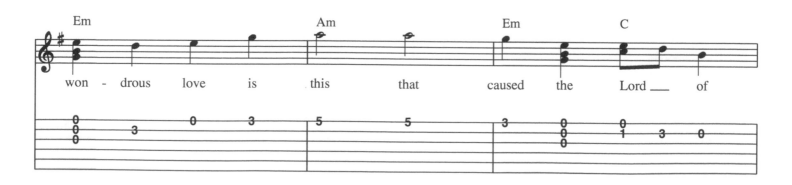

soul. What won - drous love is this, oh my soul! What

won - drous love is this that caused the Lord ___ of

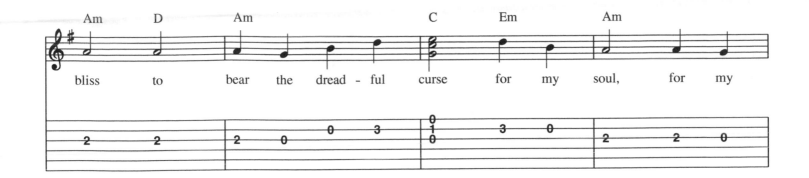

bliss — to — bear — the — dread - ful — curse — for — my — soul, — for — my

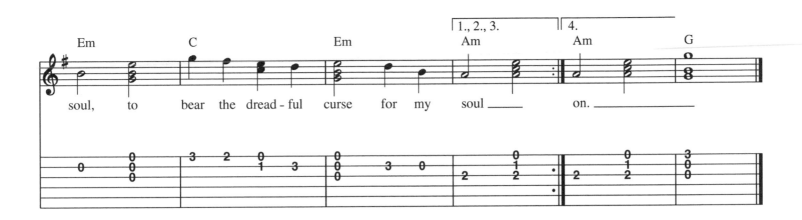

soul, — to — bear — the — dread - ful — curse — for — my — soul _____ — on. _____

1., 2., 3. **4.**

Additional Lyrics

2. What wondrous love is this, oh my soul, oh my soul.
   What wondrous love is this, oh my soul!
   What wondrous love is this that caused the Lord of life
   To lay aside His crown for my soul, for my soul,
   To lay aside His crown for my soul!

3. To God and to the Lamb I will sing, I will sing,
   To God and to the Lamb I will sing.
   To God and to the Lamb who is the great AM,
   While millions join the theme I will sing, I will sing,
   While millions join the theme I will sing.

4. And when from death I'm free, I'll sing on, I'll sing on.
   And when from death I'm free, I'll sing on.
   And when from death I'm free, I'll sing and joyful be,
   And through eternity I'll sing on, I'll sing on,
   And through eternity I'll sing on.

EASY GUITAR WITH NOTES & TAB

This series features simplified arrangements with notes, tab, chord charts, and strum and pick patterns.

MIXED FOLIOS

00702287	Acoustic	$19.99
00702002	Acoustic Rock Hits for Easy Guitar	$15.99
00702166	All-Time Best Guitar Collection	$19.99
00702232	Best Acoustic Songs for Easy Guitar	$16.99
00119835	Best Children's Songs	$16.99
00703055	The Big Book of Nursery Rhymes & Children's Songs	$16.99
00698978	Big Christmas Collection	$19.99
00702394	Bluegrass Songs for Easy Guitar	$15.99
00289632	Bohemian Rhapsody	$19.99
00703387	Celtic Classics	$14.99
00224808	Chart Hits of 2016-2017	$14.99
00267383	Chart Hits of 2017-2018	$14.99
00334293	Chart Hits of 2019-2020	$16.99
00702149	Children's Christian Songbook	$9.99
00702028	Christmas Classics	$8.99
00101779	Christmas Guitar	$14.99
00702141	Classic Rock	$8.95
00159642	Classical Melodies	$12.99
00253933	Disney/Pixar's Coco	$16.99
00702203	CMT's 100 Greatest Country Songs	$34.99
00702283	The Contemporary Christian Collection	$16.99
00196954	Contemporary Disney	$19.99
00702239	Country Classics for Easy Guitar	$24.99

00702257	Easy Acoustic Guitar Songs	$16.99
00702041	Favorite Hymns for Easy Guitar	$12.99
00222701	Folk Pop Songs	$17.99
00126894	Frozen	$14.99
00333922	Frozen 2	$14.99
00702286	Glee	$16.99
00702160	The Great American Country Songbook	$19.99
00702148	Great American Gospel for Guitar	$14.99
00702050	Great Classical Themes for Easy Guitar	$9.99
00275088	The Greatest Showman	$17.99
00148030	Halloween Guitar Songs	$14.99
00702273	Irish Songs	$12.99
00192503	Jazz Classics for Easy Guitar	$16.99
00702275	Jazz Favorites for Easy Guitar	$17.99
00702274	Jazz Standards for Easy Guitar	$19.99
00702162	Jumbo Easy Guitar Songbook	$24.99
00232285	La La Land	$16.99
00702258	Legends of Rock	$14.99
00702189	MTV's 100 Greatest Pop Songs	$34.99
00702272	1950s Rock	$16.99
00702271	1960s Rock	$16.99
00702270	1970s Rock	$19.99
00702269	1980s Rock	$15.99
00702268	1990s Rock	$19.99
00369043	Rock Songs for Kids	$14.99

00109725	Once	$14.99
00702187	Selections from O Brother Where Art Thou?	$19.99
00702178	100 Songs for Kids	$14.99
00702515	Pirates of the Caribbean	$17.99
00702125	Praise and Worship for Guitar	$14.99
00287930	Songs from *A Star Is Born, The Greatest Showman, La La Land,* and More Movie Musicals	$16.99
00702285	Southern Rock Hits	$12.99
00156420	Star Wars Music	$16.99
00121535	30 Easy Celtic Guitar Solos	$16.99
00702156	3-Chord Rock	$12.99
00244654	Top Hits of 2017	$14.99
00283786	Top Hits of 2018	$14.99
00702294	Top Worship Hits	$17.99
00702255	VH1's 100 Greatest Hard Rock Songs	$34.99
00702175	VH1's 100 Greatest Songs of Rock and Roll	$29.99
00702253	Wicked	$12.99

ARTIST COLLECTIONS

00702267	AC/DC for Easy Guitar	$16.99
00702598	Adele for Easy Guitar	$15.99
00156221	Adele – 25	$16.99
00702040	Best of the Allman Brothers	$16.99
00702865	J.S. Bach for Easy Guitar	$15.99
00702169	Best of The Beach Boys	$15.99
00702292	The Beatles — 1	$22.99
00125796	Best of Chuck Berry	$15.99
00702201	The Essential Black Sabbath	$15.99
00702250	blink-182 — Greatest Hits	$17.99
02501615	Zac Brown Band — The Foundation	$17.99
02501621	Zac Brown Band — You Get What You Give	$16.99
00702043	Best of Johnny Cash	$17.99
00702090	Eric Clapton's Best	$16.99
00702086	Eric Clapton — from the Album Unplugged	$17.99
00702202	The Essential Eric Clapton	$17.99
00702053	Best of Patsy Cline	$15.99
00222697	Very Best of Coldplay – 2nd Edition	$16.99
00702229	The Very Best of Creedence Clearwater Revival	$16.99
00702145	Best of Jim Croce	$16.99
00702278	Crosby, Stills & Nash	$12.99
14042809	Bob Dylan	$15.99
00702276	Fleetwood Mac — Easy Guitar Collection	$17.99
00139462	The Very Best of Grateful Dead	$16.99
00702136	Best of Merle Haggard	$16.99
00702227	Jimi Hendrix — Smash Hits	$19.99
00702288	Best of Hillsong United	$12.99
00702236	Best of Antonio Carlos Jobim	$15.99
00702245	Elton John — Greatest Hits 1970–2002	$19.99

00129855	Jack Johnson	$16.99
00702204	Robert Johnson	$14.99
00702234	Selections from Toby Keith — 35 Biggest Hits	$12.95
00702003	Kiss	$16.99
00702216	Lynyrd Skynyrd	$16.99
00702182	The Essential Bob Marley	$16.99
00146081	Maroon 5	$14.99
00121925	Bruno Mars — Unorthodox Jukebox	$12.99
00702248	Paul McCartney — All the Best	$14.99
00125484	The Best of MercyMe	$12.99
00702209	Steve Miller Band — Young Hearts (Greatest Hits)	$12.95
00124167	Jason Mraz	$15.99
00702096	Best of Nirvana	$16.99
00702211	The Offspring — Greatest Hits	$17.99
00138026	One Direction	$17.99
00702030	Best of Roy Orbison	$17.99
00702144	Best of Ozzy Osbourne	$14.99
00702279	Tom Petty	$17.99
00102911	Pink Floyd	$17.99
00702139	Elvis Country Favorites	$19.99
00702293	The Very Best of Prince	$19.99
00699415	Best of Queen for Guitar	$16.99
00109279	Best of R.E.M.	$14.99
00702208	Red Hot Chili Peppers — Greatest Hits	$16.99
00198960	The Rolling Stones	$17.99
00174793	The Very Best of Santana	$16.99
00702196	Best of Bob Seger	$16.99
00146046	Ed Sheeran	$15.99
00702252	Frank Sinatra — Nothing But the Best	$12.99
00702010	Best of Rod Stewart	$17.99
00702049	Best of George Strait	$17.99

00702259	Taylor Swift for Easy Guitar	$15.99
00359800	Taylor Swift – Easy Guitar Anthology	$24.99
00702260	Taylor Swift — Fearless	$14.99
00139727	Taylor Swift — 1989	$17.99
00115960	Taylor Swift — Red	$16.99
00253667	Taylor Swift — Reputation	$17.99
00702290	Taylor Swift — Speak Now	$16.99
00232849	Chris Tomlin Collection – 2nd Edition	$14.99
00702226	Chris Tomlin — See the Morning	$12.95
00148643	Train	$14.99
00702427	U2 — 18 Singles	$19.99
00702108	Best of Stevie Ray Vaughan	$17.99
00279005	The Who	$14.99
00702123	Best of Hank Williams	$15.99
00194548	Best of John Williams	$14.99
00702228	Neil Young — Greatest Hits	$17.99
00119133	Neil Young — Harvest	$14.99

Prices, contents and availability subject to change without notice.

HAL•LEONARD®

Visit Hal Leonard online at **halleonard.com**

1221
306

JAZZ INSTRUCTION & IMPROVISATION
BOOKS FOR ALL INSTRUMENTS FROM HAL LEONARD

500 JAZZ LICKS
by Brent Vaartstra
This book aims to assist you on your journey to play jazz fluently. These short phrases and ideas we call "licks" will help you understand how to navigate the common chords and chord progressions you will encounter. Adding this vocabulary to your arsenal will send you down the right path and improve your jazz playing, regardless of your instrument.
00142384 ....$16.99

1001 JAZZ LICKS
by Jack Shneidman
Cherry Lane Music
This book presents 1,001 melodic gems played over dozens of the most important chord progressions heard in jazz. This is the ideal book for beginners seeking a well-organized, easy-to-follow encyclopedia of jazz vocabulary, as well as professionals who want to take their knowledge of the jazz language to new heights.
02500133 ....$14.99

THE BERKLEE BOOK OF JAZZ HARMONY
by Joe Mulholland & Tom Hojnacki
Learn jazz harmony, as taught at Berklee College of Music. This text provides a strong foundation in harmonic principles, supporting further study in jazz composition, arranging, and improvisation. It covers basic chord types and their tensions, with practical demonstrations of how they are used in characteristic jazz contexts and an accompanying recording that lets you hear how they can be applied.
00113755 Book/Online Audio.....................$19.99

BUILDING A JAZZ VOCABULARY
By Mike Steinel
A valuable resource for learning the basics of jazz from Mike Steinel of the University of North Texas. It covers: the basics of jazz • how to build effective solos • a comprehensive practice routine • and a jazz vocabulary of the masters.
00849911 ....$19.99

COMPREHENSIVE TECHNIQUE FOR JAZZ MUSICIANS
2ND EDITION
by Bert Ligon
Houston Publishing
An incredible presentation of the most practical exercises an aspiring jazz student could want. All are logically interwoven with fine "real world" examples from jazz to classical. This book is an essential anthology of technical, compositional, and theoretical exercises, with lots of musical examples.
00030455 ....$34.99

EAR TRAINING
by Keith Wyatt, Carl Schroeder and Joe Elliott
Musicians Institute Press
Covers: basic pitch matching • singing major and minor scales • identifying intervals • transcribing melodies and rhythm • identifying chords and progressions • seventh chords and the blues • modal interchange, chromaticism, modulation • and more.
00695198 Book/Online Audio.....................$24.99

EXERCISES AND ETUDES FOR THE JAZZ INSTRUMENTALIST
by J.J. Johnson
Designed as study material and playable by any instrument, these pieces run the gamut of the jazz experience, featuring common and uncommon time signatures and keys, and styles from ballads to funk. They are progressively graded so that both beginners and professionals will be challenged by the demands of this wonderful music.
00842018 Bass Clef Edition $19.99
00842042 Treble Clef Edition $16.95

HOW TO PLAY FROM A REAL BOOK
by Robert Rawlins
Explore, understand, and perform the songs in real books with the techniques in this book. Learn how to analyze the form and harmonic structure, insert an introduction, interpret the melody, improvise on the chords, construct bass lines, voice the chords, add substitutions, and more. It addresses many aspects of solo and small band performance that can improve your own playing and your understanding of what others are doing around you.
00312097 ....$19.99

JAZZ DUETS
ETUDES FOR PHRASING AND ARTICULATION
by Richard Lowell
Berklee Press
With these 27 duets in jazz and jazz-influenced styles, you will learn how to improve your ear, sense of timing, phrasing, and your facility in bringing theoretical principles into musical expression. Covers: jazz staccato & legato • scales, modes & harmonies • phrasing within and between measures • swing feel • and more.
00302151 ....$14.99

JAZZ THEORY & WORKBOOK
by Lilian Dericq & Étienne Guéreau
Designed for all instrumentalists, this book teaches how jazz standards are constructed. It is also a great resource for arrangers and composers seeking new writing tools. While some of the musical examples are pianistic, this book is not exclusively for keyboard players.
00159022 ....$19.99

JAZZ THEORY RESOURCES
by Bert Ligon
Houston Publishing, Inc.
This is a jazz theory text in two volumes. **Volume 1 includes**: review of basic theory • rhythm in jazz performance • triadic generalization • diatonic harmonic progressions and analysis • substitutions and turnarounds • and more. **Volume 2 includes**: modes and modal frameworks • quartal harmony • extended tertian structures and triadic superimposition • pentatonic applications • coloring "outside" the lines and beyond • and more.
00030458 Volume 1 ....$39.99
00030459 Volume 2 ....$32.99

JAZZOLOGY
THE ENCYCLOPEDIA OF JAZZ THEORY FOR ALL MUSICIANS
by Robert Rawlins and Nor Eddine Bahha
This comprehensive resource covers a variety of jazz topics, for beginners and pros of any instrument. The book serves as an encyclopedia for reference, a thorough methodology for the student, and a workbook for the classroom.
00311167 ....$24.99

MODALOGY
SCALES, MODES & CHORDS: THE PRIMORDIAL BUILDING BLOCKS OF MUSIC
by Jeff Brent with Schell Barkley
Primarily a music theory reference, this book presents a unique perspective on the origins, interlocking aspects, and usage of the most common scales and modes in occidental music. Anyone wishing to seriously explore the realms of scales, modes, and their real-world functions will find the most important issues dealt with in meticulous detail within these pages.
00312274 ....$24.99

THE SOURCE
THE DICTIONARY OF CONTEMPORARY AND TRADITIONAL SCALES
by Steve Barta
This book serves as an informative guide for people who are looking for good, solid information regarding scales, chords, and how they work together. It provides right and left hand fingerings for scales, chords, and complete inversions. Includes over 20 different scales, each written in all 12 keys.
00240885 ....$19.99

HAL•LEONARD®
www.halleonard.com